D0876588

MORPHOLOGIES

SHORT STORY WRITERS
ON
SHORT STORY WRITERS

ESSAYS

Edited by
Ra Page

FRANKLIN TOWNSHIP PUBLIC LIBRARY
485 DEMOTT LANE
SOMERSET, NJ 08873
732-873-8700

First published in Great Britain in 2013 by Comma Press
www.commapress.co.uk

Copyright © remains with the authors and editor 2013
This collection copyright © Comma Press 2013
All rights reserved.

The moral rights of the contributors to be identified as the Authors of this Work
have been asserted in accordance with the Copyright Designs and Patents Act
1988.

A CIP catalogue record of this book is available from the British Library.

ISBN   1905583486
ISBN-13   978 1905583485

Supported by
**ARTS COUNCIL
ENGLAND**

The publisher gratefully acknowledges assistance from Arts Council England.

Set in Bembo 11/13 by David Eckersall
Printed and bound in England by Berforts Information Press Ltd.

Contents

Introduction:
Starting at the End

THIS COLLECTION OF essays takes its name – perhaps a little irreverently – from Vladimir Propp's *The Morphology of the Folktale* (1928, English translation 1958), a landmark text in Russian formalism that set out to identify irreducible narrative elements in 101 fairytales, from a source text of nearly 300 (previously collected by Alexander Afanasyev). Propp used the word 'morphology' to suggest a set of shared components that had emerged organically across the entire genus of Russian fairytales, the way certain bodyparts are shared, for example, across different species of insect. In this study, Propp identified 31 core 'functions' that every fairytale seemed to contain, and which obeyed a testable set of rules and variations: 'schemes handed down for generations as ready-made formulae capable of becoming animated with [...] new mood[s], giving rise to new formations.' Propp concluded his remarkable text with the claim that even contemporary literature will eventually fit into this analysis, once 'the synthesis of time, that great simplifier' has reduced it 'to the magnitude of points receding into the distance.' Even current literature, he claimed, will see its 'lines merge' with the patterns he uncovered in his country's fairytales (Propp 1968: 116).

This book doesn't quite share Propp's vaulting ambition. The purpose of asking fifteen contemporary short story writers to offer structural appreciations of their favourite past masters was *not* to uncover some unity of practice, or some single set of structures comparable to Propp's schemata. The wonder of the short story – not to mention its unique political power – lies in its pluralism, its sheer variety and flexibility as a form. Accordingly, the purpose of these essays is to foreground just such multiplicity: the many styles, shapes, structures, and techniques the short story has to offer, looking at out-of-copyright stories published in the hundred years between 1835 and 1935 – a period that arguably saw all the major story types emerge. To draw out and celebrate the idiosyncrasies of the author in question; to point readers to texts they might not have considered before; to encourage people to re-read old favourites – these are the manifest aims of this book.

However, it strikes me that attempting to squeeze the reflections of fifteen contemporary authors, and a century's worth of short stories, into a Propp-shaped matrix, in the mercifully short space of an introduction, might actually be quite fun.

It's very easy to see how short stories differ from one another. Consider any handful of examples and instantly, as a group, they start to diverge. Philip Stevick, in the introduction to his influential 1971 anthology, *The Anti-Story*, identified perhaps the most recognised partition in short story forms, between what he called 'traditional' short stories and 'classic modern' ones. In the traditional short story, Stevick asserts '*something happens*. Sherlock Holmes finds the criminal. The nice boy overcomes obstacles and marries the nice girl. That sort of thing.' In other words, the traditional story is defined by its external events. Conversely, 'in the classic modern story what tends to happen is subjective and inward' (Stevick 1971: xvii) – by which, presumably Stevick means internal revelations, the 'epiphany' as Joyce called it. Despite Stevick's deliberate simplification of the material, it's a surprisingly resilient demarcation. In Stevick's 'traditional' story, the key needed to unlock a problem and put in motion a resolution is always an external event – either one that reveals, retrospectively, a whole sequence of previously unseen events, or one that kick-starts a chain of subsequent ones leading to a resolution. In the 'classic modern' story, by contrast, the key is internal and only ever takes the form of a realisation, an unexpected change of heart that pulls us up, as readers, and makes us re-evaluate the protagonist's whole personality.

Functionally, however, Propp might question the obviousness of any distinction between a Holmesian whodunnit and a 'modern' internal story. Functions, Propp explained, are 'stable, constant elements in a tale, independent of how or by whom they are fulfilled' (Propp 1968: 21). It wouldn't matter to Propp, if the character undergoing the re-evaluation is a fairly distant walk-on villain (as in the Holmesian whodunnit), or an intimately close protagonist, whose world view and inner life the reader has been sharing (modern revelation). Functionally, both types of story are performing the same trick: a reveal.

On previous occasions, I've argued that both traditional and modern revelation stories can be grouped together under the first of Eileen Baldeshwiler's two story types: the Epical Story. I've also argued that, as well as this and her second great category, the Lyrical Story, we should consider a third: the Artificial Story (Page 2006: vii–xi).

The 'Three Types' theory goes something like this: The Epical story is defined by its deliberate withholding of a vital part of the narrative – not a subplot but a wholly conflicting 'replacing story' – which crashes into view only at the very last moment. This further-reaching 'replacing story' (either a plot, or a characterisation) is quite unexpected and yet, in hindsight, perhaps inevitable, being the only thing that could explain the earlier, unnoticed deviations from the initial 'apparent' story. In order for it to be a true revelation, this replacing story, when it comes, has to re-illuminate all that's preceded it, indeed it casts its light further – beyond the reaches of the story itself. Whether it is Holmes revealing 'who done it', in retrospect (traditional epical), or a Joycean character having an unexpected change of heart (modern epical), in both cases the reader is learning something radically new and far-reaching at the very last moment. This type of story is end-loaded.

If the Epical story has 'a decisive ending that sometimes affords universal insight', the Lyrical story, by contrast, 'relies for the most part on the open ending' (Baldeshwiler 1994: 231). Instead of focusing on plot, the Lyrical story is distinguished by its emphasis on a central, recurring image – or 'image-situation' as David Constantine puts it in his essay here – around which the narrative revolves, and from which it acquires a fluid and shifting meaning. These images 'are not symbols,' argues Constantine, 'they are not there as mere instruments, pointing to something else beyond themselves. They are moments, real concrete details around which the story's developing sense accrues, precipitates.' Examples of these lyrical images in the stories discussed here include: the evil eye in Poe's 'Tell-Tale Heart', the vision of water (and things in it) in Chekhov's 'Gusev', the eponymous flowers in Lawrence's 'Odour of Chrysanthemums', and so forth. Once established – usually in the first act of the story – the image is returned to and re-interpreted as the story progresses. Though fluid in meaning, it remains physically static: unexplained and unresolved, burning in the mind of the reader long after the story has concluded, the way a bright light might burn on the retina after it's been switched off. This type of story is front-loaded.

Finally, we have the Artificial Story, so named because it deploys a nugget of artifice at its start – that is to say, something that shouldn't be there, that through its very oddity tells us something new. As Sara Maitland explains, this unreal element is 'presented as a seamless or natural part of an otherwise realistic situation'. This unreal 'nugget' sets in motion two separate stories – the realist and absurdist – running parallel, the one illuminating the other. The master-text here is Kafka's 'Metamorphosis' of course but, as Maitland shows, its roots can be followed at least as far back as Hawthorne. Again, this type of story is front-loaded.

So how does this tripartite taxonomy stand up to the other essays gathered here?

An implication behind Stevick's initial 'traditional versus modern' distinction is that the former, plotted revelations lead the reader by the hand to the meaning of the story, whilst modern, internal epiphanies have to be decoded, in part, by the readers themselves. In other words, the reader is relatively passive in traditional stories – that these might be what Roland Barthes calls *texte lisible* ('readerly texts') – whilst the reader is more active in modern stories – what Barthes calls *texte scriptible* ('writerly texts').

Adam Roberts might have a thing or two to say about this distinction. If the reader's contribution to the meaning of a text – its '*scriptible*-ness' – is proportional to the number of gaps a story has (obliging the reader to 'enter in and fill them' as Jane Rogers puts it), then the subject of Adam Roberts' essay, Rudyard Kipling, is surely a master of the *scriptible* text. His best stories are full of gaps, very often cavernous, baffling *plot* gaps, such as those that make 'Mrs Bathurst' so mesmerising. Sometimes a gap may occur at the very climax of the story, obscuring the revelation itself, as it does in his gothic masterpiece, 'They' (where we're never quite told what's being realised in the narrator's epiphany). Is 'They' a traditional (external event) story or a modern (internal epiphany) story? The answer is both: the revelation is unspoken, and internally realised (modern), but the thing it reveals is not the true nature of the narrator's personality, but a whole other, unspoken backstory (traditional).

Stevick's distinction between the external and internal – a throwaway remark in many respects – betrays a more pervasive simplification that has enabled what we now call 'genre' and 'literary' short stories to distance themselves. Not only has this been damaging to the wider reception of short fiction it also ignores Poe's first great contribution to the field:

the primacy he placed on 'effect' over plot, character and everything else – an approach that lead directly to the very blurring of internal and external in his best work.

The partition between Baldeshwiler's higher categories – the Epical and Lyrical – seems, on inspection, just as porous. We can use the most iconic of epical story authors – one who Stevick himself mocks, Arthur Conan Doyle – to demonstrate this. Martin Edwards argues here that, unlike his literary heirs', 'Conan Doyle's aim was not so much to play a game with his readers, as to intrigue and enthrall them'. To play a game is to allow the reader to solve a puzzle before the detective solves it for them, that is to allow 'active' reading in an otherwise fixed, passive, revelation story (the possibility of a *scriptible* text collapses into a *lisible* one in the final Drawing Room scene). But to be 'enthralled' is different. It is to wonder at something unresolved, and open.

What's remarkable about many of Conan Doyle's shorts is not the cleverness of the plot being spun around us, but the simple pleasure derived from *allowing* ourselves, as readers, to be drawn in and bedazzled. We allow ourselves, for example, to be amazed by Holmes' instant character deductions even though they're effectively written backwards, with no retrospective clue-planting to enable us, the readers, to deduce them ourselves. That he can seduce us like this is only thanks to the fact that Conan Doyle, like Poe, puts atmosphere first; and atmosphere coalesces around out-of-place images and symbolic flourishes. As others have noted (Cox 2005: 23), it is Conan Doyle's red-herrings, his colourful dead-ends, that transfix us first (the factory for making artificial knee-caps, the gypsies' speckled handkerchiefs, etc). These glimpses are backed up by further-reaching images that thread through the best stories and never quite get resolved. Take this passage from the opening of 'The Five Orange Pips': 'All day the wind had screamed and the rain had beaten against the windows, so that even here in the heart of great, hand-made London we were forced to raise our minds for the instant from the routine of life and to recognise the presence of those great elemental forces which shriek at mankind through the bars of his civilisation, like untamed beasts in a cage' (Doyle 1992: 91). There can be little doubt from the importance Doyle later bestows on this storm – ultimately doing Holmes' work for him and dispatching the villain – that he intends it to carry serious metaphoric cargo, and that it draws readings out of us while remaining utterly impervious. Is it an expression of the vengeful instincts latent in civilised man that make him capable of inventing such societies as the KKK (to which the villain belonged)? Does it point to larger, global forces, slowly amassing against the British Empire, waiting for their moment? Or is it just a storm? And look what's happened now: we have started to interrogate the most traditional of epical stories, as if it were a lyrical one.

Which brings us to the Artificial story. In the wake of Kafka, more recent examples of this type might be Primo Levi's 'Magic Paint' or Adam Marek's 'Testicular Cancer vs. the Behemoth' – great examples of how a single nugget of artifice can be presented in 'convincingly realistic' terms. If we consider this nugget in terms of its structural role, however, we're struck by how many similarities it shares with the irresolvable image of the lyrical story. Both are out of place and hard to reconcile with their context. Both interact with the surrounding (realistic) story at various points, illuminating it with different meanings and interpretations each time. Perhaps the only structural difference is that, in the Artificial story, the irresolvable image is given its own plotline, the image becomes its own character, by means of surrealism or magic realism. But if we demote character, in favour of function, as Propp suggests we should, the lyrical image and the artificial nugget amount to the same thing.

So we're back where we started. All attempts to distinguish different species of short stories have collapsed in on themselves, cross-contaminated, commingled and interbred: the traditional epical with the modern epical; the epical with the lyrical, the lyrical with the artificial. Elements of all four seem to be equally present in the vast majority of short stories if we only look closely enough. In Proppian terms, all we're left with is two *functions*: the irresolvable image (front-loaded), and the all-revising revelation (end-loaded). Revelation requires its preceding counterpart, of course: misdirection (the author's misdirection of the reader, and, in many modern epicals, the protagonist's misdirection of themselves); although the term 'misdirection' makes it sound more calculating and tricksy than it actually is. So that gives us, perhaps, three functions: *image, misdirection, revelation.*

It's often been said that short stories are teleological in their form; that they continually build towards, and are forever conscious of, an ending. This ending may be a physical one – a death, a departure, a disappearance – or more simply a change, the passing of an opportunity, the end of a way of life. In a short story there isn't a great deal of time for much else in fact. When O'Brien says of Poe's most famous tales, that they 'consist almost entirely of climax', he could almost be talking about short stories generally. The 'discourse' of the story, to use a structuralist term, 'plunges us in' not so much *in medias res* as *in fine rerum* – at the end of things. 'The opening sentence is a foreclosure,' Toby Litt notes of two Kafka stories. We begin at the end, at the precipice of an ending, or indeed a few inches *over the edge of it*, whether we, or the characters, know it yet. In terms of the events and the ending they brought about, the deed is done, all is already lost, no agency on the characters' part can, or could have, averted this ending. To put it another way, the short story occupies that strange, transitory airlock between losing something and understanding what that loss means.

But how can our three functions – image, misdirection, revelation – all be squeezed into one ending, or one 'airlock' just after an ending? Lawrence's 'Odour of Chrysanthemums' is the object lesson. The sight and smell of chrysanthemums provides the lyrical image, planted at the start of the story and threading through it, blossoming into different meanings and memories with each appearance (torn at by Elizabeth's son, admired by her daughter, remembered in the buttonhole of her drunken husband, etc.). The second function here, the misdirection, is Elizabeth's seemingly complete understanding of her husband – her depiction of him as the neglectful father, the predictable drunkard. The third function, the revelation, is her sudden realisation, at the last, that she never knew him at all. 'Odour' is in many ways the perfect harmony of all three functions – overlapping, interlinking and complementing each other, organically. It's also a wondrous example of an open revelation. While so much criticism still follows the short story, because of its alleged fondness for neat, closed endings, 'Odour' shows us how a revelation can be both utterly explicit and, at the same time, indefinite: it's not clear to Elizabeth, now, who her husband ever was.

Novels have endings as well, of course, and often derive new, revelatory meanings from them. How is the short story's ending different? The answer has to do with the direction in which the ending projects its meaning. In the novel, a final revelation can only reasonably project its meaning backwards – the Rosebud effect, if you like. With a short story, the meaning of the ending is projected in both directions, backwards (illuminating an unseen plot or a misread character) as well as forwards, into the surviving future. As much as short stories are about endings (closed), they are also about the surviving of those endings (open), and what might now happen after the story finishes. As MacLeod puts it, the ending has an 'afterlife'. It poses a question of the future.

In the stories appreciated here we see a range of different types of 'airlock' emerging – different aftermaths for the story's 'present tense' to occupy: in the delirium of a deathbed, awaiting the end ('Gusev'); at home, waiting for bad news to arrive ('Odour'); visiting a house of mourning ('The Sisters'); in the weeks after a father's death, still fearing his presence ('Daughters of the Late Colonel'); two decades after a crime, waiting for the past to catch up ('Hands'); even, in Wells' 'The Star', gazing down on the surface of the Earth, as humanity awaits armageddon. Whatever the point-of-view, however close to, or distant from the suffering, the structure is still the same: the game is already up, the events of the story cannot be averted, the damage is done.

The three *functions* don't always stack neatly on top of each other, the way they do in 'Odour'.

The central, lyrical image may arrive later than usual, in the second half of the story for example, as it does in Mansfield's 'The Fly', or the image of the phone ringing in Nabokov's 'Signs and Symbols'. (It still needs to recur, of course.) Alternatively, the moment of revelation may be delayed and become separated from the plot or characterisation it reveals by many years – as it does in Anderson's 'Hands' and Dostoyevsky's 'The Peasant Marey'. Sometimes it might not even be clear what, exactly, is coming to an end. Kipling's 'Mary Postgate' seems to be layered with multiple endings: the death of young Wyndham, then of little Edna, then of the parachuted pilot. Here, as in 'Hands', the trigger for the (reader's) revelation may be situated in the present (the death of the pilot), but the real ending is, presumably, some far more intimate loss that predates the story itself. What else could have left Postgate so emotionally cold in the first place? What else could have abandoned her so permanently in her airlock? To use O'Brien's term, so 'trapped'.

Occasionally, the revelation has a positive effect, leading to further action, rather than just plot stasis, or plot ellipsis. In these cases, we see the protagonist leaving their post-plot airlock, and passing through into the next stage of their lives. This has a dramatic effect on the structure. Here, the entire story effectively severs in two, with the revelation acting as a bridge between each half. In the past: the immovable, closed plot, from which the players could not have deviated (and to which the revelation applies). In the future: a new, open story, suddenly free for the protagonist(s) to possess in unspecified ways. For this to happen, the previous, 'closed story' (the one being revealed) has to be witnessed by a bystander who then, on witnessing it, becomes the major, establishing force in the second, 'open' plot. Here, in the moment of revelation – the climactic twist in one person's story becomes a causal, imagistic starting point for the bystander's new, open story. This is the case in a surprising variety of stories. In crime stories, the bystander is the detective who suddenly transforms from being essentially a framing device, to an agent – the frame tilting into the plot itself, like a skylight swinging out into the sky. In Lawrence's 'The Horse-Dealer's Daughter', the bystander is a local doctor, Jack Fergusson, who happens to witness the revelatory, climactic act of Mabel's 'closed story': he sees this quiet, neglected woman suddenly asserting herself, attempting the ultimate act of self-definition, suicide. The revelation in Mabel's closing story becomes a seeding image in Fergusson's new, open one; Mabel's external act – of walking slowly out into a still, green pond – becomes Fergusson's irresolvable image.

Another example is Dostoyevsky's 'The Peasant Marey', where the narrator lies in his prison bunk, leafing through memories – his only form of entertainment. In one such entertainment, he suddenly remembers an incident from his childhood. In an instant he mutates from being a mere bystander to that event, to someone transformed by it, twenty years later. The act, back then, becomes the image now.

So if the plot can divide, like this, into two halves without affecting the overall short-story-ness, what else can? The central image in 'Odour of Chrysanthemums' arguably spawns a second image, in the form of Elizabeth's husband's lifeless body – the ultimate, unknowable 'other' in the universe of that story. Likewise the paired *misdirection* and *revelation* functions can themselves divide into more pairs. Fitzgerald's 'Bernice Bobs Her Hair' has a double twist: first, Bernice's movement from dull, dependent hanger-on to social superstar is reversed with the trap that her jealous cousin Marjorie sets for her; then it's reversed again with Bernice's final, symbolic act of revenge.

INTRODUCTION

Evidently, this sort of 'self-dividing' is not against the morphological rules of the short story. But the more it happens, inevitably, the less power each particular function (or function-pair) has – Poe's 'unity of effect' being a more nuanced version of 'less is more'. Bernice's final regaining of control in the Fitzgerald story is a lesser revelation than those offered by other stories considered here, if only because we've already seen Bernice taking control in the first misdirection. There's nothing new to it.

Mansfield solves this size problem in 'At the Bay', by spreading the revelations out among many characters, rather than have them all apply to one. Over twelve movements and almost as many characters, we see a scattered rhythm of misdirection and revelation working among them, like the sea crashing and receding up and down the sand. But 'At the Bay' sits at the far-reaches of what we can call a short story. It stretches Poe's unity of effect daringly, but arguably only holds together, as a single piece, by putting so much emphasis on the loss and revelation of one person in particular, namely the slightly evasive Aunt Beryl.

In most modern shorts the revelation is negative, however. That is to say it kick-starts no new action, no secondary story. Instead it leaves its protagonist (and reader) in their particular airlock *indefinitely*, with no suggestion of when, or if, they will be allowed to pass into the next stage of their lives.

So the question poses itself: while the surviving protagonist waits in this airlock (and we wait with them), what is there for them to do, other than enact the three functions: misdirect (through backstory and characterisation); share a revelation (through an unexpected act or memory); and stare at an irresolvable image? What else is there to pass the time with? Nothing, according to our present morphology. How else can a character interact with an irresolvable image, other than by staring at it?

Something is definitely missing.

To see what, we only have to consider the minimalist end of the short story spectrum. Poe's 'A Man of the Crowd' is perhaps the most paired-down story considered here, more of a proto-story, really: devoid of backstory, and therefore misdirection; devoid also of revelation, or indeed any kind of climax, and unusually linear. The 'Man' in question has no history, no name, and as the tale unfolds provides no new information at all. With all else stripped away, we see, through the narrator's eyes, the one remaining function: the irresolvable image – the man himself, unexplained, sphinx-like.

Let's consider this image… But that's the point. We can't. Poe understands this better than anyone. 'The Man of the Crowd' spells it out for us in not one but two languages: '"Er lasst sich nicht lessen" – it does not permit itself to be read' (Poe 1993: 255). Indeed he bookends the story with this phrase. Versions of it, and its surrender to the impossibility of the reading task, thread through many of the essays, and the stories they discuss, here. 'I do not know,' repeats Toby Litt throughout his essay on Kafka. 'The character's (and our) "knowing" is inseparable from an "unknowing",' is Alison MacLeod's rendering of it. Or, as the narrator of Lovecraft's 'The Colour out of Space' confesses: 'Do not ask me for my opinion, I do not know – that is all.' (Lovecraft 2002: 198)

There is something unreadable at the heart of all great short stories. The lyrical image, perhaps, or something behind it. We pretend to read it: characters hold up their personalities, like filters, to the light each image radiates, and together we interpret the colours. But remove personality altogether, as Poe does in 'A Man of the Crowd', and you effectively block the light completely, like holding a thumb up to mask the glaring sun. Then, suddenly, there in the corona, the crown around the obstruction, we see something. An activity! An event, of sorts. One that answers our rhetorical question: How can a character interact with an irresolvable image?

By rite, that's how. Ritual. A pointless, futile type of sacrament. Perhaps this is a tautological argument; being stuck in an airlock, no act can have any real consequence. A ritual is an act with no consequence, thus ritual fills the space. But it's also all you can do, dramatically speaking, with an irresolvable image (once you've tired of interpreting it), and all it can do in return.

Poe's 'Man of the Crowd' enacts a ritual, wandering ceaselessly round and round the same patchwork of streets, and it is all the narrator can do to match him, commune with him in the same senseless march. How we interpret this ritual is up to us. But once we notice it and start looking for it in other stories, we see it everywhere. In Elizabeth and her mother-in-law's cleaning of the body in 'Odour of Chrysanthemums'. In the mathematician's purely academic calculation of the time left for mankind in 'The Star'. In the majestic sacrament that closes the life of 'Gusev', delivering him to a home other than the one he'd longed for.

The ritual is as essential to the lyrical image as the misdirection is to the revelation. The functions pair off together, like binary stars. In Sherwood Anderson's story, the inexplicable central image is Biddlebaum's own hands – inexplicable even to himself. In the unending airlock of his days, all he has left to do with them is perform a ritual: 'A few stray white bread crumbs lay on the cleanly washed floor by the table; putting the lamp upon a low stool he began to pick up the crumbs, carrying them to his mouth one by one with unbelievable rapidity […] The nervous expressive fingers, flashing in and out of the light, might well have been mistaken for the fingers of the devotee going swiftly through decade after decade of his rosary.' (Anderson 1992: 51)

So, it seems, we have arrived at two pairs of functions for the short story: (i) the misdirection, (ii) the revelation, (iii) the irresolvable, out-of-place image, and (iv) the ritual. These functions can be in any order so long as (i) appears before (ii) and both apply to the same thing (plot or characterisation), and (iii) first appears before (iv) and then reappears offering conflicting interpretations.

This is all just a bit of fun, of course. Propp's 'fairytale functions' are far more detailed and specific than what I've offered here for the short story. At best, Propp might call our four, assembled elements 'function groups', and going into any more detail would probably pull down my whole house of cards analysis. Having had our bit of fun, though, it's interesting to note that Ali Smith found something quite similar to our scheme, in the teasingly brilliant 'clue words' planted at the start of James Joyce's first story. These three words – *paralysis*, *gnomon* and *simony* – could perhaps be mapped onto our suggested morphological 'setting' and our two pairs of function groups, respectively: 'paralysis' denoting the airlock; 'gnomon' meaning the part of the sundial that points one way while 'revealing' something in another direction with its shadow (misdirection and revelation); and 'simony' being someone who trades in sacred things, after Simon Magus who tried to buy the power of laying on of hands – in other words, the secularised 'sacred object' and 'laying on of hands' of the image and the ritual.

At the start of my bit of fun, I deliberately ignored one of Stevick's two throwaway examples for the traditional epical – the romantic hero story: nice boy overcomes obstacles to marry nice girl. Both its linearity and, frankly, its optimism seem anathema to the short story. It's a story type Propp would recognize, of course, and countless novelists. The folklorist Alan Dundes points out that the final function in Propp's fairytale schemata is 'The Wedding', whilst his first function is 'One of the members of the family is absent from home.' For the fairytale, then, perhaps the meta-function – the overarching function of the whole tale – is the wedding ritual: the formation of a new family from the demise of an old one (Propp 1968: xiii). If I could play this morphological game for one last round, it would be to suggest, that the meta-function for the short story is not the wedding, but the funeral. The funeral and our surviving it.

Sara Maitland

on

Nathaniel Hawthorne

EDGAR ALLAN POE described Nathaniel Hawthorne as, 'a man of the truest genius... We look upon him as one of the few men of indisputable genius to whom our country has as yet given birth.' Herman Melville dedicated his masterpiece, *Moby Dick*, to Hawthorne as his inspiration. D.H.Lawrence admired his 'marvellous allegory, so deep and so complete.' The contemporary critic Harold Bloom has written of Hawthorne as one of three greatest American prose writers (with Henry James and William Faulkner) and explicitly includes some of his short stories as well as his most famous novel, *The Scarlet Letter*, in his judgement.

Nathaniel Hawthorne was born in 1804 in Massachusetts. He was influenced as a young man by Ralph Waldo Emerson's Transcendentalist philosophy and he married (very happily) Sophia Peabody, a Transcendentalist artist. Apart from a brief period in Europe, where he was US Consul in the administration of his college friend President Franklin Pierce, he lived in New England, wrote, and supported himself and his family with a job in the Customs Office.

He wrote seven novels and a substantial body of short stories. But, with many of the short stories it can be very difficult on a cursory reading to understand what the fuss was about. They can feel rather old fashioned and moralistic, loosely constructed and overwritten. They do not fit neatly into any contemporary category of fiction and often seem a bit morbid or merely weird. Hawthorne wrote in what Poe described as a 'peculiar' style. (By 'peculiar' Poe did not mean 'odd' or 'eccentric' but the older and more specific sense of 'particular-to-an individual', what we might call 'strongly voiced'.)

However I am going to argue that the fault is in our reading not Hawthorne's writing. I believe these are not simply experimental stories, but that the experiment has since ripened into rich fruit. Hawthorne used the central tropes and techniques of Magic Realist (or Magical Realist) fiction about 100 years too soon.

Literary Magic Realism (as opposed to Magic Realism in visual art) has been defined as fiction where some 'magical' (not possible in a material, physical universe operating under the scientific laws as we know them) elements are presented as a seamless or natural part of an otherwise realistic situation. Magic Realism has been marked by some distinct literary techniques, which distinguish it from fantasy, horror, surrealism or science fiction: these include intertextuality, fantastical elements, excess ('plenitude' or 'baroque') of disorienting detail, authorial reticence (both expository and ethical), social critique and the refusal of closure.

What follows is a reading of perhaps Hawthorne's most famous short story, 'Young Goodman Brown', in the light of these categories. Of course Hawthorne wrote other short stories but 'Young Goodman Brown' epitomises his approach in so many ways that it seems worth focussing on it.

INTERTEXTUALITY
Here is the opening paragraph of 'Young Goodman Brown':

Young Goodman Brown came forth at sunset into the street at Salem village; but put his head back after crossing the threshold, to exchange a parting kiss with his young wife. And Faith, as the wife was aptly named, thrust her own pretty head into the street, letting the wind play with the pink ribbons of her cap while she called to Goodman Brown.

No-one is going to be surprised that Hawthorne, product of puritan New England begins by referencing the Bible (King James translation, inevitably). 'Came forth' is an inescapably biblical turn of phrase (a fact that would have been even more blatantly obvious to his New England contemporaries where even profound sceptics were more likely to become Unitarians than secularists), but in fact the reference is more subtly nuanced. In Psalm 19:5 the morning sun 'cometh forth like a bridegroom from his chamber and rejoiceth like a strong man to run its race'. But this bridegroom came forth at sunset, and far from rejoicing hesitates immediately and puts his head back. Throughout the story, Hawthorne uses a great many 'old fashioned' (for his own time, not simply ours) expressions – including the 'quoth' that Poe took up shortly afterwards in his famous Raven poem – and they almost always come freighted with ironic biblical reference.

Salem village though is not, I think, so much biblical reference as something more immediate and personal, although it equally sets up gloomy expectations of dealing with the supernatural. Salem was of course the location of the witchcraft trials of 1692 and 93. It was also a point of personal reference for Hawthorne, who was born and grew up in Salem, a direct descendent of the town's founding families. His own great-grandfather was not simply one of the judges at those monstrous trials; he was the only one of them who never repented of his role in the deaths of over 25 women. (Hawthorne as a young adult added the 'W' to his name, probably to separate himself from association with Judge Hathorne.) Since by the mid-1830s it was generally recognised just how hysterical and unjustified these trials had been, making Salem about the only point of actual 'social' realism undercuts any too literal or realist interpretation of the story.

Meanwhile although the wife is 'aptly' called Faith, she is wearing 'pink ribbons' and 'thrusts' herself into the street. It is not true that New England puritan women only wore black – in fact, black was disapproved of because black dye was very expensive and therefore extravagant (they favoured dark blues and greens), but virtuous women did not wear pink, or frivolous 'ornamentation' of any kind.

Thus, in just four, superficially innocent lines, Hawthorne has cross-referenced an extraordinary range of texts and social conventions to open a destabilised, 'unreliable' and potentially sinister tale. And it goes on – before the bottom of the first page Hawthorne evokes a forest so clearly drawn from the German Fairy stories that were beginning to circulate, and bearing not much relationship to 'real' local woods. This trick of deploying details from other popular genres is a favourite device – for example, Hawthorne often locates stories in vaguely Italian locations or gives his characters Italian sounding names to pick up on the Gothic 'sensation stories' (gothic horror plus romantic drama) which were still massively popular in the mid-nineteenth century. His first short-story collection was titled *Twice Told Tales* (1837) – although, in fact, none of the stories were retellings of genuine old tales – to suggest the timeless 'antique' flavour of what he was attempting. Over and over again he achieves an almost subliminal resonance by this very subtle cross-referencing of quite common and open texts.

FANTASTICAL ELEMENTS

The whole concept of a witches' Sabbath is sufficiently 'fantastical' to modern readers for me not to need to explore this element in detail; but all Hawthorne's short stories are marked by the imposition of such elements on basically mundane people. In 'The Birth-Mark' a perfectly beautiful woman is disfigured by a facial deformity which cannot be described; in 'Rappaccini's Daughter' the pure maiden is so toxic that her breath kills plants; the hero of 'The Artist of the Beautiful' manufactures a butterfly through extremely hard work, but these elements – fantastical and metaphysical – remain random events within stories that are convincingly realistic in many other respects; they are not the ghost stories of Poe or the science fiction of Mary Shelley, or the horror tales of Bram Stoker, it is the random mixture of domestic and fantastical that will barely reappear until the Magic Realist novels of the next century.

EXCESS

Most contemporary Magic Realist writers offer excess in the form of descriptive detail: Tristessa's palace in Angela Carter's *The Passion of New Eve* would be an excellent example of this tendency. It is here perhaps that Hawthorne is least like the more conscious users of the genre – his 'plenitude' is carried more in the writing itself, the extravagance of his grammar and his baroque syntactical anachronisms.

Edgar Allan Poe described Hawthorne's writing style as 'purity itself', but it is a little hard for the modern reader to perceive this: 'purity' has come to mean 'simplicity'. Hawthorne's writing is excessive – and disorienting in its excess. He is excessively keen on the wild regions of punctuation (especially exclamation marks and dashes), on exclamatory repetition, and on adjectival exuberance. I think this is the most alienating factor in Hawthorne's writing and can put off the innocent reader. It is probably worth remembering that this sort of linguistic extravaganza was much more common and acceptable in the early nineteenth century – it seems to have represented 'sensibility' and depth of emotional engagement in a way that fiction simply does not do anymore. Sensing that a sort of baroque tone was vital to his fiction, Hawthorne was obliged to exaggerate the available devices. Clearly Poe understood what Hawthorne was up to.

RETICENCE

A strong characteristic, arguably the defining characteristic, of Magic Realism is the authors' refusal to 'explain away' the fantastical aspects of their narrative, or to comment – explicitly or implicitly – on the credibility of their imaginary worlds. Marquez has said of *One Hundred Years of Solitude*, 'My most important problem was destroying the line of demarcation that separates what seems real from what seems fantastic.'

In 'Young Goodman Brown' and elsewhere, Hawthorne is clearly wrestling with this issue. He was writing in a society that was both almost bizarrely credulous and at the same time looking for 'scientific' explanations. The intelligentsia of the nascent United States was struggling with a new model of the imagination, drawn from Romantic idealism and with challenging concepts of individual freedom; it was trying to take on board the new biblical criticism while still enmeshed in Calvinist theology and ethics; and did not yet have the tools or vocabulary of psychology or psychoanalysis to assist them. The idea of the 'omniscient author' was far from dead – the author was supposed to explain. Readers did not want authorial reticence; they desired precisely the demarcation Marquez describes. (This problem was not confined to the USA – in 1847, the year after Hawthorne published his second collection of short stories, *Mosses from an Old Manse,* Emily Bronte published *Wuthering Heights* which confronts much the same question.)

Hawthorne deals with this in a distinctly different way from Marquez: rather than 'destroying the line of demarcation' he problematises it. A number of his stories end by asking the question explicitly – 'Had Goodman Brown... only dreamed a wild dream?' and then answering it ambivalently, reticently – 'So be it if you will, but, alas!' (*sic.)* – there were real consequences for him. The question is not rhetorical – it is a deliberate and tactical withdrawal on the part of the author. It asks the question and then declines to provide the wanted answer (or indeed any answer).

SOCIAL CRITIQUE

Magic Realism has been a genre of the left – politically engaged in destabilising and decentring the discourses of power. In this it has always shown its affinity to classic fairy stories and folk tales, as opposed to grander mythologies. (This has become less obviously true recently as diverse writers have adopted many of the tropes of Magic Realism to less radical ends.) Its origins in South America have emphasised this, but many of the non-Latin American Magic Realists have followed this lead – Rushdie in *Satanic Verses* and Morrison in *Beloved,* for example, use the genre to challenge post-colonialism and racism; Carter to interrogate gender; and early Paul Magrs (*Marked for Life* and *Does it Show?)* to challenge class.

It is worth remembering that the United Sates in the first half of the nineteenth century was a post-colonial society, dealing with many of those tensions. Hawthorne's short stories share the moral compass of Magic Realism. At the most basic level, Goodman Brown is identified with the agricultural workers, over and against the morality of those in power. When Satan (if it is Satan) suggests that the authorities are among his friends, Goodman Brown declares that he has 'nothing to do with the governor and council; they have their own ways and are no guide for a simple husbandman like me.' But Hawthorne's social critique is more complex and refined than this simple statement reveals. 'Young Goodman Brown' is frequently read as an attack on the hypocrisy of New England Puritanism and the repressive and dishonest effects of self-satisfaction, judgement and the cult of public purity. And so it is, but it is equally a savage denunciation of Transcendentalist philosophy which was gaining ground among intellectuals and progressives. Transcendentalism taught the inherent goodness of all human beings, and maintained that society and all social institutions, especially organised religion and political parties, contaminated the natural perfection of individuals. This romantic, quasi-mystical optimism was repellent to Hawthorne – and it was this aspect of the philosophy that led him and Melville to question Emerson's sanity. 'Young Goodman Brown' is as much a critique of this sentimental perfectionism as it is an assault on Calvinistic theology and morality.

REFUSAL OF CLOSURE

In *Le Plaisir du texte* (Pleasures of the Text) (1973) Roland Barthes contrasts the 'satisfaction' of closure to the *jouissance* (bliss) of the open or unresolved ending. In short stories, particularly nineteenth century ones, the emphasis has traditionally been strongly on the former – hence the popularity of the 'twist' ending in the late nineteenth century, exemplified by writers like Maupassant, O.Henry and, later, Somerset Maugham. Modern short stories, even though the plotted 'twist' or 'surprise ending' is regarded as rather vulgar, tend to have sharp endings, clear conclusions, reposeful closure. Writers have developed tight framing devices which mark out the fictional space and then release the reader back into the 'real' world. Hawthorne repudiates any such finality, as many Magic Realist writers do and at first reading this makes the ending of many of his stories, including 'Young Goodman Brown', feel loose and unsatisfying – as though he did not quite know when or how to stop. But look again, because what he does is extremely crafty. He brings the story to within a paragraph of the ending. He asks a question – 'Had Goodman Brown fallen asleep in the forest and only dreamed a wild dream of a witch-meeting?' which could be the ending and then he opens it out again and hands it back to the reader – 'Be it so if you will'. This could provide proper closure, though of a different kind. But no, he opens it out a second time, and hustles the reader through the whole of the rest of Goodman Brown's life in less than twenty lines and buries his wrecked protagonist without giving the reader any space to resist, nor offering any comfort.

And to achieve this expansive evasive ending Hawthorne manages an extraordinarily bold sleight of hand. Remember those pink ribbons: they appear in the first paragraph, and twice more on the first page. In a story singularly devoid of bright colours (even the fires are dark flamed) they impose themselves on the reader's attention. At almost the middle of the story, Goodman Brown sees a cloud passing overhead and hears the voices of shrieking women, one of them possibly Faith's – and from the cloud a pink ribbon 'lightly fluttered down through the air'. Goodman Brown seizes it. Later when he returns home Faith is still sporting her pink ribbons. For most writers the pink ribbons would have been a neat little plotting device, a proof: either she is missing one and he still has the one he seized in his pocket (the events had material reality) or he looks for it and it is not there (the events were a dream or fantasy). Hawthorne simply ignores the question. He has drawn our attention irresistibly to these ribbons – but we have been duped. Their sole purpose is to emphasise that he will not 'explain' or offer the easy satisfactions of closure.

I could go on. There are other tropes common to Magic Realism, like its tendency to require readers to engage at an intensified emotional level while simultaneously questioning their own relationship to the text; its continual combinations of uneasy or inharmonious elements – 'hybridity'; its summoning of the sense of 'collective unconsciousness'. All of these (and more) can be demonstrated in Hawthorne's short stories.

'Young Goodman Brown' is an extraordinary, prophetic work of fiction, written a full century before its time. My main point in trying to read the story in this way is to underline the profoundly experimental, open nature of short stories themselves. After the publication of *Mosses from an Old Manse* in 1846, Hawthorne's publisher (and close friend) encouraged him, as too many publishers still do, to develop one of his short stories into a novel. We can be glad that he did and that Hawthorne knuckled down to the task because *The Scarlet Letter* is, for me, perhaps the finest example of the nineteenth-century 'romantic' novel. I love it and it has insured Hawthorne's noble place in the literary canon. But let us be clear – it is in many ways highly conventional, it makes no major narrative challenge and can be slotted tidily into its place. What Hawthorne did pull off in his short stories he could not transfer to the longer form.

I believe that great short stories have this 'forecasting' aspect. It is one major reason why they matter.

Ten Essential Stories

'My Kinsman, Major Molineux' (1831)
'Young Goodman Brown' (1835)★
'Wakefield' (1835)
'The Minister's Black Veil' (1836)
'The Man of Adamant' (1837)
'The Hollow of the Three Hills' (1837)
'The Birth-Mark' (1843)
'Rappaccini's Daughter' (1844)
'The Artist of the Beautiful' (1846)
'Ethan Brand' (1850)

Sean O'Brien

on

Edgar Allan Poe

In one sense, and in great measure, to be peculiar is to be original, and than the true originality there is no higher literary virtue. This true or commendable originality, however, implies not the uniform, but the continuous peculiarity – a peculiarity springing from ever-active vigor of fancy – better still if from an ever-present force of imagination, giving its own hue, its own character to everything it touches, and, especially, self impelled to touch everything.
– 'Twice-Told Tales' (Poe 2003: 387–397)

POE WAS INCLINED to be categorical in his remarks as a critic, as he shows in this extract from his essay on Nathaniel Hawthorne, where he uses a limiting judgement on Hawthorne's stories as an opportunity to promulgate the general truth of an artistic principle which clearly derived from Poe's own practice and circumstances. Eliot was to do the same and by doing so create an authority which Poe did not live to enjoy.

Poe's peremptory impatience with most of his contemporaries may have been a matter of temperament, but it also reflects the permanently embattled conditions of a life and career that almost make the plight of his admirer Baudelaire seem mild. Poe struggled to serve two masters: the betterment

11

of American literature, in which he succeeded; and the need to make a living, in which he died still trying, beset on the one hand by alcoholism exacerbated by his sense of family responsibility, and on the other by the hostility of the largely mediocre establishment to which he opposed himself. The need to work, and the yet more powerful need to serve a distinctive literary vision, were tasks for which he was both heroically ready and physically unfitted. The extremity of his vision and the economy he advocated and sought to perfect are, by sombre irony, wholly apt to the conditions in which he had to operate. He remained an artist where most others would have been reduced to the status of hacks, while the art itself often embodies the desperation of imaginative insomnia endured in one of Piranesi's imaginary prisons: Poe's characters often live in a condition of intolerable hyper-consciousness

If the fact that Poe was pre-eminently a writer of tales, a miniaturist who perfected a certain kind of short story – the tale of obsession – makes perfect sense in terms of his life, what makes his fiction particularly interesting, given his gifts of compression, is that it seems far superior to his poetry. Atmospheric and accomplished as the poems are, they remain in thrall to a kind of Romanticism whose day was almost past when Poe was writing. They lack the intensity and energy of the tales, though both are intended to fit Poe's insistence that the best works are those that could be read at a single sitting, and in which the unity of a single completed effect could be discerned. In the stories brevity becomes a kind of prosody in itself, replacing the layer of formality given by rhyme, metre and stanza.

When he moves on to consider the shortcomings of other American contemporaries in 'Twice-Told Tales', Poe praises Washington Irving's *Tales of a Traveller* but with this serious reservation: 'In many of them the interest is subdivided and frittered away, and their conclusions are insufficiently *climactic.*' In their various ways, some of Poe's most famous stories – 'The Tell-Tale Heart', 'The Cask of Amontillado', 'The

Fall of the House of Usher' and 'The Facts in the Case of M.Valdemar', for example – seem to consist almost entirely *of* climax. A relatively unsuccessful story, 'The Oval Portrait', usefully exhibits this tendency to an almost mechanical degree: the narrator breaks into a lonely castle and in the bedchamber spends the night in contemplation of a compellingly lifelike portrait of a young woman. Perusal of a convenient catalogue of the paintings in the castle reveals that the young woman died during the cruelly extended sitting the painter required to perfect the work. 'The Oval Portrait' seems to reveal an imaginative algorithm, without convincing us that there is much at stake or persuading us of the reality of this young woman, to whom we have scarcely been introduced. Poe's work is of course full of more successful depictions of beautiful, dead, near-dead and undead women, but even in its failure 'The Oval Portrait' in particular looks forward to Wilde's *Dorian Grey*, sideways at Browning's 'My Last Duchess' and forward again to 'The Red Shoes' and *The Collector*, all of which substantiate some the possibilities sketched by Poe, most of which permit themselves a far more extended treatment of the theme.

'The Oval Portrait' recalls a description of some of Byron's work as seeming to be written while dressing for dinner, though dinner was not always easy for Poe to come by. For the stories that *do* triumphantly succeed, it is first of all important that the reader is persuaded for the duration that the story-world is the world's entirety – that there is nowhere else to be, that the tales' milieux are not variations on a recoverable norm, but are all that is and has ever been the case, miniature worlds as constrained as the teeming, overheated brain itself which can no longer distinguish inner from outer phenomena. Poe's claustrophobia is imperious – '*self compelled to touch everything*' – and there are few writers who can match his power to immediately generate a sense of context. For example:

For the most wild, yet most homely narrative which I am about to pen, I neither expect nor solicit belief. Mad indeed would I be to expect it, in a case where my very senses reject their own evidence. Yet mad I am not – and very surely I do not dream. But to-morrow I die, and today I would unburden my soul.
– 'The Black Cat' (Poe 1993: 189)

I must not only punish but punish with impunity. A wrong is unredressed when retribution overtakes its redresser. It is equally unredressed when the avenger fails to make himself felt as such to him who has done the wrong.
– 'The Cask of Amontillado' (Poe 1993: 202)

Above all was the sense of hearing acute. I heard all things in the heaven and in the earth. I heard many things in hell. How, then, am I mad? Hearken! and observe how healthily – how calmly I can tell you the whole story.
– 'The Tell-Tale Heart' (Poe 1993: 221)

In each case the teller exerts the same inescapable control as Coleridge's Ancient Mariner, though in Poe's case there is for the reader the additional uncomfortable sensation of the story having been phantasmally in progress for some time before we become aware of it. We as readers are somehow complicit as citizens of the fictive worlds from which the narrators reach out as in familiar address, confident that we will understand what they disclose and recognize the logic they command or have at some time commanded. These methods reflect Poe's insistence, in 'The Philosophy of Composition'(1846) that 'It is only with the *denouement* constantly in view that we can give a plot its indispensable air of consequence, or causation, by making the incidents, and especially the tone at all points, tend to the development of the intention.' 'Tone' is a word long indispensable to the criticism of poetry, and one also important to Henry James's attempts to assure the status of fiction as art. And with 'tone' goes another of Poe's articles of faith, the importance of 'effect', with all it implies about formal unity.

Once we are privy to the meticulous reasoning of the madhouse, from then on it is all lurid intensity, often sustained by Poe's manipulation of the presiding past tense to make events and sensations suffocatingly *present* and at the same time to prove them sealed against escape. The stories often read like traps in themselves.

Poe is undeniably an acute observer and dramatist of abnormal psychological states, and this is an important reason why we read him, but this power does not entirely account for the sense of exposure and confinement that the stories create in the reader. That this should be so depends to a significant degree on things largely absent from the worlds Poe creates – work, family and ordinary life among them (although these were things that, in life, he tried desperately to sustain). Compare a later masterpiece of the tale of terror, one that involves the supernatural as Poe does not, Elizabeth Bowen's 'The Demon Lover'. Bowen's story requires an everyday world of bourgeois comfort and sobriety – admittedly one made strange by the Second World War – from which the mild, decent, middle-aged heroine is to be dislodged and finally snatched away by the figure in the title as he rises from the graveyard of the First World War into the innocent here and now. For Poe there seems to be no such place as the everyday. This can be illustrated by a relatively untypical story, 'The Man of the Crowd'. Here the narrator, idly amusing himself in town, is struck by the appearance and conduct of an old man. The stranger wears an expression of 'absolute idiosyncrasy' which brings to mind 'ideas of vast mental power, of caution, of penuriousness, of avarice, of coolness, of malice, of blood-thirstiness, of triumph, of merriment, of excessive terror, of intense – of extreme despair. I felt singularly aroused, startled, fascinated... Then came a craving desire to keep the man in view – to know more of him.' The narrator follows the old man all night in his wanderings in the city. It turns out that the sinister flâneur suffers from a form of the problem diagnosed by Pascal as the inability to sit quietly in one's room. The old man cannot bear to be alone and is the more emphatically alone because of his insatiable appetite for the illusory company of the various crowds who pass through the city.

This is a genuinely modern story, describing the city as Baudelaire knew it, with its vast crowds wandering through desolation. Such is the story's modernity that Poe avoids the over-simple kind of equation that mars 'The Oval Portrait'. We know that the narrator is, albeit unwittingly, becoming a member of the demonic old man's tribe of restless solitaries, another glutton of the crowd, but he is not 'the same' as the old man, for no one is the same as anyone else, and the narrator's own observations of types, classes and professions tend paradoxically to emphasize this by evoking a mass anonymity.

In 'The Man of the Crowd', the mere activity of walking becomes a deranged and endless ritual, a mapping of anxiety through an inescapable labyrinth of its own devising, in the place where religion would at one time have been found. Ritual produced by obsession is often at the core of Poe's stories. The walling-up of Fortunato in 'The Cask of Amontillado' is more than an action: it is a performance whose victim is also to be its audience. In this Poe contributes crucially to the idea of the killer as a kind of aesthetic aristocrat of torment, most famously embodied in the character of Hannibal Lecter and thereafter exploited to exhaustion in innumerable books and films about serial killers whose cellars and tunnels are the stages for site-specific dramas. The torments of the narrator in 'The Pit and the Pendulum' partake of a ritual character deriving from the sacrificial ideology of Catholicism and apparent in many other examples of torture both real and fictional to this day, in which the ordeal of torture is intensified by its orderliness and formality. In 'The Case of M. Valdemar' the experiment on the dying man, to see (perhaps) if consciousness survives death, is conducted by a mesmerist whose entire practice is ritualistic, occurring at the uneasy frontier between science and superstition. And in two of Poe's most strikingly Gothic tales, 'The Masque of the Red Death' and 'The Fall of the House of Usher', the locations, Usher's pile and the palace of Prince Prospero, seem invested in their very fabric with a sense of the enactment of rites: the world of these two stories conducts a perpetual funeral for the future. In this sense Poe's story-worlds function as invocations of the powers that will destroy some of their central characters, or as verbal altars on which imaginative sacrifice is performed.

This degree of through-composition, with its tendency to confer agency on the texture and symbolism of the work itself, is perhaps more immediately characteristic of poetry than prose. Dickens, a contemporary of Poe's, likewise lends himself to this kind of totalizing reading, and his work, like Poe's, might seem to have anticipated the appetites of later literary criticism and theory. The completeness of a poem has as much to do with musical organization as with an avowed theme (this implied distinction is of course misleading but necessary). Like other significant literary artists such as Eliot and Yeats, Poe framed a theory. He commended brevity, unity and compression, and perhaps also implied the displacement of familiar meaning by intensity of apprehension – and sought to demonstrate the inescapable rightness of his own practice. The surviving evidence of his tales bears out the wisdom of his methods and the durability and originality of his art.

Ten Essential Stories

'Ms. Found in a Bottle' (1833)
'The Fall of the House of Usher' (1839)
'The Man of the Crowd' (1840)★
'The Oval Portrait' (1842)★
'The Pit and the Pendulum' (1842)
'The Masque of the Red Death' (1842)
'The Black Cat' (1843)★
'The Tell-Tale Heart' (1843)★
'The Facts in the Case of M. Valdemar' (1845)
'The Cask of Amontillado' (1846)

Jane Rogers

on

Fyodor Dostoyevsky

IN CONTRAST TO his novels, Dostoyevsky's stories remain surprisingly little-known. This may be partly due to there being very few of them – collections are always based upon one of the novellas, either *Notes from the Underground* or *The Eternal Husband,* with a handful of short stories thrown in to bring the volume to a respectable length. It may also be due to the fact that some of the early stories are rather sketchy. But I would argue that the later (post 1862) stories are as brilliantly achieved as the novels, and display in miniature some of the obsessions, themes, and techniques of the novels, alongside real virtuosity in handling the short story form. Several of them are also very funny: there is humour in the novels, often of an absurd or embarrassing nature, but in the stories it tends to be more fantastical and satirical – to be mocking human folly in a way which is very reminiscent of Gogol. In Dostoyevsky's 'Bobok' the dead in their graves bicker unrepentantly and vie for social superiority; in 'Another Man's Wife' a series of farcical events leads to a jealous husband hiding under an unknown lady's bed, where he finds another gent who is also there by mistake. The two argue in furious whispers while the lady's aged husband puzzles over the noise, and when the lady's yapping lapdog threatens to reveal them, our hero promptly strangles the tiny dog and secretes it in his pocket. In 'The Crocodile', the protagonist is swallowed alive by the crocodile, and pontificates daily, to an admiring audience, from within the beast's belly.

Others of the stories are more realistic, and 'The Meek One' in particular explores themes which are central to the great novels: guilt, shame, pride, love, and the conflicts and contradictions seething in a mind under terrible pressure. 'The Meek One' is narrated in the first person by a pawnbroker whose sixteen-year-old wife has just jumped from a window and killed herself. The pawnbroker is a social misfit, a proud critic of fashionable society, who nevertheless longs to be accepted by it; he shares these characteristics with the narrator of *Notes from the Underground*. But while the narrator of *Underground* is constantly worrying about what others think of him, second-guessing the reader's opinion, and contradicting himself, the pawn broker is only now – after his wife's suicide – becoming aware that his view, his system, may not have been the best one. Now, in a self-acknowledged state of confusion and despair, with the body lying on his kitchen table, he attempts to tell their joint story chronologically, from the moment she first entered his shop with cheap tat to pawn. His apparently artless outpouring turns out to be remarkably carefully structured. Dostoyevsky has divided it into two chapters consisting of ten sections, each between three and five pages long, and in each section the power passes from one character to the other, as a crude summary will show:

CHAPTER 1

1. Pawnbroker gives girl money and helps her. He has power.

2. Girl hesitates before accepting his proposal, despite the fact that the alternative is marriage to an evil old shopkeeper who has already worked two wives to death. She has power.

3. They are married and the girl attempts to show kindness

and affection, which he ignores, treating her with cold sternness; he has power.

4. He realises with horror that his cold treatment has made her hate him: she has power.

5. He eavesdrops as she has a tryst with another man, and drags her home in shame. Having uncovered her disloyalty, he has power.

6. In the night she seizes his gun and points it at him; he lies helpless, pretending to sleep, aware of her movements. She cannot bring herself to fire, and lets the gun drop. 'She was conquered.' In this crisis, power shifts, from her to him.

CHAPTER 2

7. She is sick and crushed, almost dies, lives like a mouse. He has power.

8. He overhears her singing, she has forgotten he is at home. He realises she doesn't care about him at all, and throws himself at her, confessing how much he loves her. She has power.

9. She apologises to him and says she will be a true wife, he is happy and believes he has achieved his aim of breaking her and then making her love him for the right reasons. He makes excited plans for their future. She kills herself. Power shifts, from him to her.

10. Resolution: he understands that she despised him and killed herself rather than live to be tormented by him. Power remains with her.

To summarise, there are five sections of turn-and-turn about power, then a dramatic crisis (attempted murder) where he seizes power from her: then two sections of turn-and-turn about power, and a dramatic crisis where she seizes power from him (suicide); followed by a resolution. And this is a story which, as Dostoyevsky himself says in his foreword, is written to appear as the realistic ramblings of a grief-stricken man: 'The process of the narrative goes on for a few hours, with breaks and interludes and in a confused and inconsistent form: at one point he talks to himself; then he seems to be addressing an invisible listener, a judge of some sort. But so it always happens in real life. If a stenographer had been able to eavesdrop and write down everything he said, it would be somewhat rougher and less finished than I have it here; still, it seems to me that the psychological structure would perhaps be just the same.' (Dostoyevsky 1994: I, 678).

Apparent artlessness is achieved by the most carefully structured art. Raymond Carver's story 'Blackbird Pie', unreliably narrated by an historian whose wife is leaving him for reasons he cannot understand, is so similar in design that it would be interesting to know if Carver modelled it on 'The Meek One'. Telling the tale of a relationship from only one partner's point of view makes for a powerfully engaging story; the gap, where the woman might have related her side of things, hooks the reader into collaboration with the writer, as the reader tries to work out what the wife must really have been thinking and feeling (as opposed to what her husband insists she was). 'I never hesitated for a moment and poured cold water upon all her raptures. That was essentially what my idea amounted to. To her transports I replied with silence. Benevolent silence, no doubt, but all the same she soon realised that we were different and that I was an enigma,' claims the narrator, outlining his plan to make his young wife love him for himself (Dostoyevsky 2001: 228). The carefully composed and highly dramatic structure of this story, based on reversals, shows in miniature a fine example of the architecture of Dostoyevsky's novels: but in the novels, multiple voices and multiple storylines twist and turn and echo and conflict with and counterpoint one another. Here in the short story, intensity is achieved by the single focus of the lone narrator's point of view. (A similar intensity is engendered in *Notes from the Underground*, written twelve years earlier, and again restricted to a single first-person voice.)

It's frustrating to read a great writer in translation, but a lot better than not reading him at all. The English editions I've read differ alarmingly in places, and most significantly in 'The Meek One' when, just before the suicide, the maid says to the girl, 'Master ought to have asked your pardon a long time ago, Madam' (Dostoyevsky 2001: 257) or: 'You should have come to the master long ago, ma'am, to ask forgiveness' (Dostoyevsky 2008: 313). Since the maid is a touchstone for good sense and kindliness in the story, it matters very much who she thinks should have asked forgiveness of whom. There are points where the translators agree, fortunately, and then we get a glimpse of the powerful echoes Dostoyevsky has set up in the language of the story. When the girl is first married to the pawnbroker he shows no affection and is *stern*. It is his arbitrary, power-seeking stern coldness which first alienates her. When he finally apologises and hurls himself passionately at her in Ch 2, she stares at him with *stern* astonishment. The repeated use of the word *stern* ironically links his original manipulative affectation, with the genuinely cold response it has engendered in her.

Dostoyevsky's skill with language is most evident, in translation at least, in his dialogue – which is always vividly dramatic, and revealing of character and social status. The economy and humour of several of the stories depends upon this. In 'Bobok' the corpses chatter, each according to his or her station in life, condemning themselves by their own triviality. Here the society lady bemoans the fact that she is buried next to a lowly shopkeeper. Their spat is interrupted by a servile flunkey who is toadying up to a dead general.

'We are equal in sin before God's judgement,' [intones the shopkeeper].

'Equal in sin,' the deceased lady mimicked scornfully. 'Don't you dare say another word to me!'

[Flunkey] 'Still, the shopkeeper is doing as the lady says, your Excellency.'

[General] 'And why should he not do as she says?'

'As we all know, your Excellency, because of the new order down here.'

'What new order do you mean?'

'Well, you see, your Excellency, we have, so to say, died.' (Dostoyevsky 1994: 175)

Humour is generated by the contrast between the venial, worldly desires of the dead, and the constant reminders of the condition of their bodies; an ancient and rotted privy councillor drools over the giggling corpse of a fifteen-year-old girl. The conceit of the story is that the dead retain the ability to talk for a limited period, three months or so, gradually losing this facility as they rot. Far from using this last chance to talk of anything important, they bicker idiotically. The 'bobok' of the title means 'a bean' and this is the final, absurd, repeated utterance of a corpse 'almost entirely decomposed', on the brink of that permanent silence towards which all of us are heading.

One of the key preoccupations in the novels is the exploration of pride and shame; hypersensitivity to the opinions of others, and a dreadful despair at appearing foolish or inferior in their eyes. This is treated to farcical effect in 'A Nasty Anecdote', when a self-important official who has already had too much to drink decides to honour a lowly clerk in his office by dropping in uninvited to the clerk's wedding party. The serfs have only recently been liberated, and educated men are eager to show their ability to relate to the lower orders. Grandly he attempts to engage the gawping bride in conversation, and condescends to address several of the guests. Initially cowed into silence by his presence, the guests gradually become rowdy. A series of increasingly excruciating incidents culminates in a drunken guest yelling out truthfully, 'You came to flaunt your human-ness! You interfered with everyone's merrymaking. You drank champagne without realising it was too expensive for a clerk who makes ten roubles a month.' The official drinks even more to cover his embarrassment, and ends up collapsing face-first into a bowl of blancmange. Being too vomitingly drunk to be sent home, and too important to sleep in anything but the best bed, he is installed in the marital bed while the bride and groom make do with a table-top. This collapses under them before matrimonial duties can be completed, making a racket that wakes the household. Humiliation in public, at a party or dinner, is a recurring motif in both the stories and the novels: Mr Golyadkin (*The Double*) is made a laughing stock after he sneaks into a ball from which he has already been excluded; in *Notes From the Underground* the narrator is mocked and humiliated at the officer's farewell dinner party, where he is an unwelcome and drunken guest, and in the short story 'A Little Hero', the eleven-year-old narrator is constantly mortified by the public attentions of the ladies at the house party they all attend.

'A Nasty Anecdote' is a strong contender for most embarrassing story in the world (and cries out to be filmed starring Steve Coogan). It also evidences what Mikhail Bakhtin described as the chief characteristic of Dostoyevsky's novels; 'polyphony', the presentation within one work of 'a plurality of consciousnesses, with equal rights and each with its own world' (Bakhtin 1984: 6). Here the initial point of view is that of Pralinsky, the self-important official, increasingly frantic and mortified up to the point at which he collapses dead drunk. Then the point of view shifts to his lowly clerk Pseldonymov, the groom, whose side of the story is established with great economy: his impoverished background, his ant-like tenacity in trying to build a place in the world for himself and his beloved mother; his bride's dislike of him which he will endure for the sake of the house her father will give them; his knowledge that his life has been ruined by this evening because he understands that from now on the official can do nothing but persecute him at work. The final section shifts back to Pralinsky's viewpoint, revealing his hangover, his remorse and mortification (he takes to his bed for eight days) and finally his return to work, still dogged by shame and distress. Use of both points of view allows us to see both men are vulnerable and, in their way, tragic: both suffer horribly. And the intensity of that suffering is made all the more poignant by the ludicrous circumstances in which both men are humiliated.

'The Peasant Marey' provides a great contrast to this; short, and avowedly autobiographical, simply and seriously related, it charts a shift in understanding thanks to an illuminating shaft of memory. Structurally, and in tone, it could not be more different from 'A Nasty Anecdote'; but again it reveals hidden depths in characters who appear initially as stereotypes.

In prison in Siberia, fearing and hating the drunken violence of the common criminals around him, the narrator suddenly remembers a childhood incident when he was terrified of being chased by a wolf in the woods. A peasant, working in the field, comforted him. 'I remember… that thick finger of his, smeared with earth, with which he touched my twitching lips so gently and with such shy tenderness. No doubt, anyone would have done his best to calm a child, but something quite different seemed to have happened during that solitary meeting; and if I had been his own son, he could not have looked at me with eyes shining with brighter love.' (Dostoyevsky 2001: 94) This peasant is owned like a chattel by the boy's family, yet treats him with almost motherly love and gentleness. Memory of his kindliness transforms the narrator's view of the vicious criminals around him: 'That rascal of a peasant with his shaven head and branded face, yelling his hoarse drunken song at the top of his voice – why, he too may be the same sort of peasant as Marey: I cannot possibly look into his heart, can I?'

The past illuminates and transforms the present, reinforcing, but this time very simply, Dostoyevsky's great theme, that all men and women have their own stories inside their own hearts, and that all are of equal importance.

Dostoyevsky's ability to inhabit a wide range of points of view extends not only to separate individual characters in his fiction, but also to the host of contradictory voices he often presents within a single consciousness. His fictional heroes argue endlessly with themselves, and allied to this comes a fascination with doubles and doubling. This is first explored in the novella *The Double* (1846), where the government clerk Golyadkin is dogged by a double who is his exact lookalike, and even works in his department and shares his name. Golyadkin senior is full of vacillating self doubt; his double appears confident, malevolent, and intent on bringing about the downfall of the original. Yet he also seeks Golyadkin senior's help, and Golyadkin at times feels a close bond of friendship with him. The reader, drawn into Golyakdin senior's point of view, is invited to empathise with every humiliation and reversal he suffers. But is the Double a real man, or a product of Golyadkin senior's disordered mind? (which of course, makes him real enough). At one point the terrified Golyadkin even begins to see numerous multiples of himself – 'with every step he took, every time his foot struck the pavement, here sprang up, as if from under the ground, another exactly and completely identical Mr Golyadkin, revolting in his depravity' (Dostoyevsky 1973: 230). The theme of disintegrating identity, warring fragments within a single psyche, and schizophrenic instability is explored and developed obsessively and repeatedly in Dostoyevsky's fictions, both long and short. Opposite tendencies within a character may be personified, as in *The Double,* or may simply tear a man apart from within, as in the short story 'A Faint Heart', where the protagonist is so ecstatically happy at becoming engaged that he becomes deeply depressed by his own unworthiness, and ends in an asylum. In *Crime and Punishment* it is never entirely clear whether the detective Porfiry Petrovich is actually a part of Raskolnikov's own divided psyche or a separate entity; the Devil who torments Ivan Karamazov is a figment of his own feverish imagination, but has a physical presence in his room; in *The Eternal Husband* the cuckolded spouse haunts the adulterous protagonist as if conjured into existence by his own guilt. Although the two men are enemies, there are also moments of tender love and kindness between them (as between the two Golyadkins); one minute Pavlovich is tending the ailing Velchaninov with hot plates and tea, and the next he is standing over his sleeping body wielding a razor.

Repeatedly, characters dream that they are about to be killed, only to open their eyes and find a figure with a gun or knife standing over them, like the pawnbroker in 'The Meek One'. Dreams, premonitions, hauntings, being inhabited by multiple and contradictory voices – these are common experiences for characters in both Dostoyevsky's stories and novels. And indeed, it would seem, for Dostoyevsky himself. There is a moment of self-mockery in his journalistic column *A Writer's Diary* where he includes a letter purporting to come from 'a Certain Person', the narrator of the story 'Bobok' (i.e. a character created by Dostoyevsky). The Certain Person is highly critical of the behaviour of journalists, and describes their frantic rivalry. (That is to say, the rivalry of Dostoyevsky himself with his peers.) 'You two,' writes the Certain Person, 'have already leapt at each other, mouths foaming with rage, and are pulling at each other's hair.' Here the Editor (ie. Dostoyevsky) adds a dry footnote to this description of himself, by himself: 'The Editor finds this picture somewhat exaggerated.' (Dostoyevsky 1994: 202)

It is the sense of shifting sands, of the passionate conviction and yet utter unreliability, instability and inconsistency of 'character' in fiction, which fascinates me both as a reader of Dostoyevsky, and as a writer. The world viewed from one person's point of view (whether written in the first person or as third person restricted point of view) is always going to be unreliable – but unreliability is all we have, and I think it was through reading Dostoyevsky that I first really grasped that and grasped how a writer might portray it.

As I have begun to write more short stories, I've found the unreliable first-person voice is a gift to work with, because the reader is obliged to enter in, and fill the gaps. Dostoyevsky's writing inspires and energises me, and I come back to it again and again, especially if I catch myself writing a stereotype, a puppet whose opinions and behaviour are fixed like a rictus grin. Nikki Black, in *Island*, was rescued from being pathetic by my taking a good dose of the narrative voice of *Notes from the Underground*. Reading two sentences of Dostoyevsky is an electric shock to set my brain running again.

In his ability to get under the skin and reveal the humanity of the meanest and most ludicrous of his characters, the Dostoyevsky of the short stories equals the Dostoyevsky of the novels: what is fascinating about the stories is the economy, and variety of styles (from fable to memoir to cautionary tale to farce to realistic tragic monologue) with which he accomplishes this.

Ten Essential Stories

'Another Man's Wife' (1848)
'White Nights' (1848)
'A Christmas Tree and a Wedding' (1848)
'A Little Hero' (1849)
'A Nasty Anecdote' (1862)★
'The Crocodile' (1865)
'Bobok' (1873)★
'The Meek One' (1876)★
'The Peasant Marey' (1876)★
'The Dream of a Ridiculous Man' (1877)

Brian Aldiss

on

Thomas Hardy

IF YOU GO up the hill by Long Ash Lane, along what's now known as the A37, you will come upon the partly dream county of Wessex. Once on a time, Wessex was an Anglo-Saxon kingdom, actual until the Norman Conquest. Now Wessex is the territory of the poet and novelist, Thomas Hardy. And very picturesque and bygone it seems in our fast-moving age.

Hardy for some of us is first and foremost a poet. For others, he is a major English novelist. For a smaller number of readers he is author of that mighty play, *The Dynasts*, an intense drama of the Napoleonic Wars, rarely performed.

Hardy also wrote short stories. On my shelf full of books about Hardy's writing, few critics discuss his stories. However, there is Kristin Brady's splendid *The Short Stories of Thomas Hardy* (1982) in which she says that the mosaic-like unity of the collection suggests a wide range of human experience. As we see, J.I.M. Stewart, in his volume, *Thomas Hardy, A Critical Biography* (1971) has a chapter on 'Minor Fiction', and singles out the story 'The Fiddler of the Reels', from the collection *Life's Little Ironies*, for our consideration.

Indeed, this is an interesting tale about a noble young woman, Car'line, who is overwhelmed by the music of a wandering minstrel – when the sounds of music were hardly

31

a daily event, as now. Car'line turns down an offer of marriage from Ned, a plain honest working man, only to write to him four years later to say yes, she does wish to marry him after all, if he will have her. Ned agrees to have her. Car'line turns up with an illegitimate child, a little girl, begotten by the aforesaid fiddler. Ned marries Car'line despite her rakish behaviour. Then the fiddler comes and steals his little daughter away.

It is an engrossing tale, unlike yet like life. The husband, Ned, a working man, needs a job, and travels up to London to find one. Car'line cannot resist the fiddler, or his exotic music; and here the background to the tale offers us a sketch of the first railway line to London, where poor passengers sit in open trucks for the journey. In London, we are given a glimpse of the Great Exhibition of 1851 (exhibiting the works of industry of all nations).

These are some of the features we encounter more than once amid often rather lengthy stories in this group of noble dames. The need to work, aristocrat versus commoner, marriages going wrong – or failing to happen – disapproving parents, an illegitimate child and, in particular, the liklihood that things are never going to work out as one hopes.

Such is essential Hardy...

There are four volumes of short stories, *Wessex Tales, Life's Little Ironies, A Group of Noble Dames*, and *A Changed Man and Other Stories*. Some of these stories were written between novels, and in indeed often tend to
ramble on as if they hoped to grow up into novels.

We encounter an instance of this in the first story of *Wessex Tales* entitled 'The Three Strangers', a tale of ingenuity, where the three named men all meet at a cottage one evening, without realising that they are enemies – in fact, they are a criminal and his pursuer and a victim. It feels like a very long story, with the ingenuity rather laboured.

Some of the tales seem like précis for novels never written, as they may have seemed to Hardy himself.

Yet in the collection, *A Group of Noble Dames*, there is one story in particular, presented as told 'by the Rural Dean', which is still, after all these years, pointed and of contemporary interest. This is the story of Dame the Third, 'The Marchioness of Stonehenge', whom we, the readers, know as Lady Caroline. A beautiful and admired grand lady indeed.

Noble titles meant something important to Hardy – not that such considerations have yet entirely died away. In *Tess of the D'Urbervilles*, we recall, the family name is a corruption of the title born by Sir Pagan d'Urberville, who came over to England with William the Conqueror. Grand indeed!

When we first meet our Lady Caroline, she has been – the Rural Dean tells us as much – courted, flattered and spoilt, and is satiated by constant praise. In contradictory fashion, she centers her affections on a plain young man of humble birth, son of the parish clerk. Lady Caroline's fancy was possibly stimulated by her finding that there was a girl in the village already in love with this young man, never named. Caroline and the young man have a romance, followed by a secret marriage.

Later, matters become difficult. The young husband is slipping away from his grand home one night, anxiously, when a spasm overcomes him. He falls to the ground and dies. So what shall widowed Lady Caroline do? She grieves, yes; she wishes, nevertheless, that her secret husband had died in his own cottage.

That night, she drags his dead body away in secret, to leave it at his cottage door. She needs to keep her marriage to a commoner secret; so she seeks out Milly, a woodman's daughter, who had once been in love with the now defunct lad.

An elaborate plan is hatched between the two women. This is Wessex of legendary days, remember. Milly should declare that she had been secretly married to the deceased.

Some force is implied. Milly unhappily agrees and accepts Caroline's secret wedding ring.

However, Milly's feelings change with time; she becomes proud to be taken for the dead man's widow. Lady Caroline pays her for the subterfuge.

Later, the two women meet in the churchyard. Now Caroline wants the pretense retracted and truth told of her secret marriage. Here the author of this complex tale says, 'There is a limit to the flexibility of gentle-souled women'.

Milly refuses to change her pose as widow-woman: 'I am truly his widow. More truly than you, my lady!'

To which Her Ladyship responds that she does love her dead husband still. They argue, there among the gravestones. Caroline pities her rival. But now she reveals that she is pregnant − pregnant and due to marry an old nobleman. So the two women do not quarrel, as well they might have done; they come to an arrangement instead. Lady Caroline and her mother go away to stay in London; there Milly joins them. After a year, Milly returns to her village with the baby, Caroline's child, to a cottage of her own, funded by Caroline and her mother.

After three years, Caroline marries the Marquis of Stonehenge. There follows a placid life. No child is born of this marriage. Meanwhile, Milly's little boy, as she considers him, grows up and thrives. At the age of twenty, he enlists in the cavalry and gains promotion.

But Caroline − now Marchioness Caroline − hears of her son's progress and becomes interested. Her old Marquis husband dies, to leave her alone and without progeny.

She visits a neighbouring town when troops were marching on parade. Troops march throughout Hardy's tales, from 'The Trumpet Major' to the tricky Sgt Troy in *Far From the Madding Crowd*. Lady Caroline thinks she recognises her son because of a likeness to his dead father. Her motherly instincts are awakened. She falls into furious debate with herself, the upshot of which is that she goes to visit Milly in her cottage and demands that Milly should give the gallant offspring soldier back to his rightful mother.

'Flesh and blood's nothing!' exclaims Milly with, as it says, 'as much scorn as a cottager could show to a peeress'.

So the soldier son is called into their presence. His manner towards Caroline is merely respectful. The alternatives for his choice of mother are put to him.

The soldier prefers things to remain as they have been. He makes two points. Firstly, that Caroline cared little enough for him when he was weak and feeble: why should he go to her now that he is strong? Milly always cared for him, and he loves her. She will always be his mother and he her son. Secondly, just as Caroline was once ashamed of his father, so is he now ashamed of her.

The Marchioness is distraught. She begs for a kiss. He obliges, coldly.

From that day onwards, Caroline begins to die. Reckless of the world's opinions, she lets her story be known and refuses the consolations of religion.

We come to the end of this brilliant story, The Rural Dean now steps forward to sum up. An honest affection can be demeaned by class-division. Lady Caroline deserves some pity; but there is no pathos like the pathos of childhood, where a child is not wanted.

As we might expect, the Dean makes no mention of Hardy's fascination with the upper crust, together with his envy and dislike of it.

This tale takes the best part of sixteen pages to unwind, Nowhere does Hardy play better on the pains of love, of secret love and secret parenthood. We recall that there is a rumour, never resolved, that young Hardy enjoyed a love affair with one Tryphena Sparks. What bearing this might have on the tale of the Marchioness of Stonehenge cannot be determined. What we do witness is Thomas Hardy's mastery of the pains of childhood, of poverty, and, with its secrecies, of love itself. All of this brilliantly carried out in a brief and memorable story.

In 1913, the year before the First World War commenced, when much of the past, good, bad or indifferent was swept away – and with them those trysts at ancient earthworks, those muskets, those lost villages – Hardy's *A Changed Man* was published, containing what he calls 'a dozen minor novels'.

The longest of these 'novels', or more accurately 'novellas', is 'The Romantic Adventures of a Milkmaid' – yet another overlooked masterpiece that deserves an essay of its own. In it, the not-so-simple country girl, Margery Tucker, falls in love with a Baron: a clever story of bygone days. Now we have fewer milkmaids, while scheming barons go under other names. You should read that story too.

Ten Essential Stories

'The Honourable Laura' (1881)
'Interlopers at the Knap' (1884)
'The Withered Arm' (1888)
'Barbara of the House of Grebe' (1890)
'The Marchioness of Stonehenge' (1891)★
'The Fiddler of the Reels' (1893)
'An Imaginative Woman' (1894)
'A Changed Man' (1900)
'The Grave by the Handpost' (1897)
'The Romantic Adventures of a Milkmaid' (1913)

Martin Edwards

on

Arthur Conan Doyle

THE DUALITY OF Arthur Conan Doyle's character reflected the two sides of Victorian society. A pillar of the establishment, knighted for services to the Crown during the Boer War, Doyle was a doctor of medicine who played first class cricket and campaigned for a series of unpopular causes, as well as a writer whose work earned worldwide admiration. Yet he possessed a powerful and morbid imagination, and owes his enduring fame to his creative use of dark visions to conjure up memorable characters, and some of the most unforgettable – and sometimes deeply disturbing – stories in the history of English literature.

'English literature', yes, but Doyle was a proud Scot. He shared a fascination for the macabre with his fellow countryman Robert Louis Stevenson, who captured the split nature of the seemingly respectable Victorian personality in *The Strange Case of Dr Jekyll and Mr Hyde*. A year after Stevenson's novella appeared, Doyle published *A Study in Scarlet*, introducing the brilliant consulting detective Sherlock Holmes.

Holmes' odd and sometimes sinister habits (soon expanded to include injecting himself with cocaine) made a stark contrast with the straightforwardness of the sturdy ex-soldier, John H. Watson, who narrated Holmes' exploits with a mixture of bewilderment and admiration with which readers readily identified. Despite the originality of the stories, Doyle was to some extent writing about what he knew. Holmes' startling deductive technique was based on the methods of the Scottish medical lecturer Dr Joseph Bell, while Watson was, like Doyle, a general practitioner.

The Sign of Four followed three years later, again enjoying modest success, but Doyle was still learning his craft. A strong influence was Edgar Allan Poe, who inaugurated the detective story with 'The Murders in the Rue Morgue'. The relationship between Poe's detective, Dupin, and the unnamed narrator of the three tales about him, was the model for the Holmes-Watson pairing. Doyle's masterstroke was to humanise his Jekyll and Hyde duo in a way that Poe did not, and perhaps could not.

Doyle's breakthrough came when he wrote a series of short Holmes-Watson stories for the recently established monthly magazine *The Strand*. In an astonishing burst of creative energy, he dashed off half a dozen, which proved an instant success. Like the cricketing bowler he was, he had found his length. Whereas Wilkie Collins and Sheridan Le Fanu had published successful crime novels, such as *The Woman in White* and *Uncle Silas*, in the mid-nineteenth century, Doyle's talents and methods, like Poe's, were better suited to the short form.

Why was this? Doyle's taste for the macabre supplies part of the answer. He had a knack of dreaming up strange and mysterious scenarios, but resolving the puzzles through Holmes' rational detective work presented a challenge in terms of narrative structure. He struggled to rise to the challenge in longer stories. *A Study in Scarlet* and *The Sign of Four* are burdened by lengthy flashbacks which militate against suspense, and frustrate readers by keeping Holmes off-stage for long stretches. The same structural flaw damages the final Holmes novel, *The Valley of Fear*. Even *The Hound of the Baskervilles*, with its dazzling premise, that a sinister spectral hound is responsible for a savage murder on fog-bound Dartmoor, is uneven, with Holmes out of the picture for too long.

Doyle hit his stride with his first short story about Holmes. 'A Scandal in Bohemia' opens with one of the most quoted lines in detective fiction: 'To Sherlock Holmes, she is always *the* woman.' Although the woman in question, the opera singer Irene Adler, never reappeared in the canon, she made a sufficient impression on readers of succeeding generations to have figured in countless Sherlockian spin-offs. Watson plays a more active part than in the first two novels, and this story stands alone as the solitary account of Holmes experiencing defeat. All that 'A Scandal in Bohemia' lacked was a strong puzzle about crime.

Doyle remedied this at once with 'The Red-Headed League'. When Holmes says to Watson, 'you share my love of all that is bizarre and outside the conventions and humdrum routine of everyday life', Doyle knew his readers shared it too, especially when they experienced it a safe distance, through fiction. Holmes introduces Watson to his latest client, Jabez Wilson, a pawnbroker whose only extraordinary feature is his head of fiery red hair. A seemingly trivial aspect of Doyle's gift for creating character was his flair for coming up with odd names that stick in the mind: Sherlock Holmes, of course, Enoch Drebber in the first novel, Thaddeus Sholto in the second, Jabez Wilson and countless others.

Wilson affords Holmes an opportunity to indulge in a wonderful example of bravura deduction: 'Beyond the obvious facts that he has at some time done manual labour, that he takes snuff, that he is a Freemason, that he has been in China, and that he has done a considerable amount of writing lately, I can deduce nothing else.' Such showmanship delighted readers. It might not be central to the story, but it was the icing on the cake.

Doyle takes care, however, to ensure that Holmes' deductions are not all superfluous to the plot. The reference to Wilson's writing is highly relevant. Wilson's obliging and under-paid assistant Vincent Spaulding has directed the pawnbroker's attention to a newspaper advertisement on behalf of 'The Red-Headed League', offering a well-paid sinecure (funded by the estate of an eccentric millionaire) to a Londoner with red hair. Wilson obtains the lucrative but absurd role, which involves being confined to the League's office and copying out *Encyclopaedia Britannica*, but after eight weeks, the League is dissolved suddenly and without explanation, and the man who hired him vanishes without trace.

Watson is bewildered, and Holmes settles down to reflect on the puzzle — it is 'a three-pipe problem'. This throwaway line demonstrates Doyle's genius for the telling phrase of the kind that quickly became familiar to his readers, and an integral part of the appeal of his fiction (Mark Haddon's *The Curious Incident of the Dog in the Night-Time*, for instance, takes its title and inspiration from a classic exchange in 'Silver Blaze'). Having mulled things over, Holmes inspects the pawnbroker's premises, and beats the pavement outside with his stick. He speaks to Spaulding, and when Watson questions him outside, explains that he wished to see the knees of the young man's trousers. Holmes declines to explain himself, so ensuring that suspense builds until the forces of justice contrive an underground encounter with a suave villain, grandson of a Royal Duke, and a product of Eton and Oxford.

This drawing-out of the mystery is commonly found in traditional detective stories, in order to keep a surprise back to the end, but runs the risk of alienating readers. The technique is more convincing with Holmes than his successors (other than, perhaps, Agatha Christie's Hercule Poirot, whose methods were influenced by Holmes') because Holmes' fondness for mystification and uttering enigmatic remarks is so plainly in keeping with his idiosyncratic personality.

The solution to Jabez Wilson's puzzle is not complex,

but that does not matter. A short story affords little scope for elaborate explanations. Doyle cleverly pre-empts any sense of anti-climax by having Holmes note that 'the more bizarre a thing is, the less mysterious it proves to be.' As a result, he achieves a level of storytelling perfection that he (let alone other detective story writers) seldom matched in the rest of a crime writing career that continued for more than three decades.

Doyle's knack of coming up with distinctive titles is illustrated by 'The Five Orange Pips', a story notable for an intriguing problem, and a device that has spawned innumerable Holmesian pastiches. Watson begins his narrative by describing his extensive records of his friend's cases, and says that the year 1887 alone furnished 'the adventure of the Paradol Chamber, of the Amateur Mendicant Society, which held a luxurious club in the lower vault of a furniture warehouse' and several others, alluded to in such tantalising fashion that generations of readers have yearned to find out more.

Baroque adornments of this kind, together with the unmistakable character names, and the astounding feats of deduction, enrich the stories, and their pungent flavour is complemented by evocative prose, as with Watson's vivid account of the storm lashing 'great, hand-made London' when John Openshaw turns up at Baker Street, on the recommendation of Major Prendargast, whom Holmes saved in the Tankerville Club Scandal. Openshaw explains that both his uncle and his father were found dead in separate incidents, shortly after receiving envelopes each containing five orange pips and marked 'K.K.K.' Now Openshaw himself has received a similar inexplicable communication, instructing him to 'put the papers on the sundial.' Holmes advises Openshaw to obey the command without delay, but shortly afterwards the young man is found drowned near Waterloo Bridge. Holmes solves the mystery of the orange pips, but justice is finally meted out to the killers not by Holmes or the legal establishment, but by an act of God.

The outcome is contrived, but the story's other elements are so compelling that this scarcely matters. Conan Doyle was not writing elaborate whodunit puzzles of the type for which Christie later became renowned. There is never a gathering of suspects in a library before an unlikely culprit is revealed, a method that became familiar in detective novels published during the 'Golden Age' of detective fiction between the two world wars. Conan Doyle's aim was not so much to play a game with his readers, as to intrigue and enthrall them.

'The Speckled Band' is a 'locked room mystery', in the tradition of 'The Murders in the Rue Morgue'. Holmes and Watson are visited by a shivering, terrified young woman called Helen Stoner. She is an heiress who lives with her brutal stepfather, the last surviving member of the Roylott family of Stoke Moran. Her sister Julia died at Stoke Moran in a state of terror, her last words, 'Oh, my God! Helen! It was the band! The speckled band!' This is the most effective example in nineteenth century detective fiction of 'the dying message clue', a device which became popular during the Golden Age, and was a trade mark of the American cousins Frederic Dannay and Manfred Lee, who wrote together as Ellery Queen.

Julia met her end in a locked room, and an inquest failed to establish the cause of death. Did she die of fear, and why does Doctor Grimesby Roylott (another marvellously evocative name) insist that Helen sleep in the same room that Julia occupied? Helen presents Holmes with a baffling confection of clues to dark deeds at Stoke Moran: mysterious whistles at night, an inexplicable metallic clang, possibly made by a bar from the room's shutters, a redundant bell-pull, the presence of a band of gypsies befriended by Roylott, and Roylott's passion for Indian animals, including a baboon and cheetah which roam his estate.

'When a doctor does go wrong,' Holmes remarks, 'he is the first of criminals.' This was long before Crippen, Buck

Ruxton and Shipman, but Doyle knew his own profession, and equally acute insights are scattered throughout his writings. Roylott is among the most memorable villains in detective fiction, immensely strong, repellent in appearance, and utterly ruthless. But he finds, as Holmes says with grim satisfaction once the mystery is solved, that 'violence does, in truth, recoil upon the violent, and the schemer falls into the pit which he digs for another.' Holmes acknowledges he is indirectly responsible for Roylott's death, but 'I cannot say that it is likely to weigh very heavily upon my conscience.' Here he is setting a pattern for fictional detectives who took it upon themselves to do justice, above all when the machinery of the legal system failed to do so. Again, this is a notion which became popular in the Golden Age – even Hercule Poirot commits a murder in one novel – underlining the extent and enduring nature of Doyle's influence upon the genre.

Doyle's mastery of the short story form is not confined to the Holmes canon. 'The Lost Special' and 'The Man With the Watches' boast conspicuous Holmesian touches, while Doyle was able to give free rein to his near-obsession with unspeakable acts in his tales of terror. He was proudest of his historical novels, but they carry the excess baggage of research and period detail, whereas the picture he creates of the last hours of Madame de Brinvilliers in 'The Leather Funnel' is all the more horrific because it leaves gaps for the reader's imagination to fill.

'Lot No.249' illustrates his ability to tease and fascinate from the opening words: 'Of the dealings of Edward Bellingham with William Monkhouse Lee, and of the cause of the great terror of Abercrombie Smith, it may be that no absolute and final judgment will ever be delivered.' Smith has given his account, and there is some corroboration from others – but can he be believed? Wryly, Doyle suggests that most people will reckon it more likely that Smith's brain, although outwardly sane, 'has some subtle warp in its texture' than that something profoundly unnatural might have taken place in 'so famed a centre of learning and light as the University of Oxford.'

A secluded turret in 'Old College' is home to three young students: Smith, Lee and Bellingham. Smith knows little about either Lee or Bellingham prior to a conversation with his friend Jephro Hastie. Lee is, according to Hastie, a gentlemanly fellow, but there is 'something damnable… something reptilian' about Bellingham, who is engaged to Lee's sister. Bellingham is fat and unprepossessing, but a gifted linguist, specializing in Eastern tongues.

Shortly afterwards, Smith hears a strange noise coming from Bellingham's room, later followed by a hoarse cry. Lee seeks his help, saying that Bellingham is ill, and once he is inside the room, furnished with countless Egyptian artefacts, Smith sees a giant mummy, 'a horrid, black, withered thing, like a charred head on a gnarled bush.' Bellingham recovers, and Smith develops an unexpected liking for him.

Soon, however, Smith is troubled by a sequence of unsettling events. Is Bellingham telling the truth when he claims he keeps a dog, which nobody has seen? What is the nature of the brute that attacked Bellingham's enemy, Long Norton? Why does Monkhouse Lee insist that Bellingham's engagement to his sister must be ended, and why does he urge Smith to change his rooms?

When Lee narrowly escapes from drowning, Smith becomes convinced that devilry is afoot behind closed doors in Bellingham's set of rooms. The build-up to the climactic scenes is suspenseful, although modern readers will guess what is going on at a relatively early stage. In part, however, this is a sign of Doyle's success – 'Lot No. 249', drawing on the then current craze for Egyptology, became the first of many to feature a reanimated mummy.

An amputating knife is put to work at the end of 'Lot No. 249'. Conan Doyle had worked as a ship's surgeon, and was well aware of the horror instilled by the threat to sever part of a living creature's body. Amputations and disfigurements recur in his work, for instance in 'The Engineer's Thumb', a Holmes story whose casual brutality seems rather shocking today. In 'J. Habakuk Jephson's Statement' (a mundane title in stark contrast to Doyle's melodramatic and highly influential 'explanation' of the mystery of the *Mary Celeste*), the sinister Septimus Goring seeks revenge for a series of racial atrocities, including the mutilation of his own hand 'by a white man's knife.'

A year after publishing 'Lot No. 249', Doyle returned to the theme of mutilation and disfigurement in 'The Case of Lady Sannox', a story of revenge as *explicitly* gruesome as anything he wrote, even though once again not a single human being dies. Gripping from start to finish, this story is noticeably shorter than 'Lot No. 249' and most of his other tales. Its effect depends on a single plot twist, and Doyle employs brevity deliberately, along with pace, to ensure the reader has no time to anticipate the shocking outcome of a vain and brilliant surgeon's decision to accept an offer of easy money.

When the story was published in the collection *Round the Red Lamp*, a critic in *The Spectator* was appalled: 'We cannot conceive any volume in which 'The Case of Lady Sannox' ought to appear at all. It is a story – we believe, morally impossible – which makes the victim of a great crime even more detestable than the perpetrators of it' (*The Spectator*, 16 Feb 1895: 22). The reviewer also disliked 'Lot No. 249', but admitted that was at least an ingenious exercise of the morbid imagination, whereas he felt that 'It is very doubtful how far any imaginative attempt to improve on the occasional gruesomeness of actual life is at all desirable.' For him, 'The Case of Lady Sannox' was beyond the pale. What provoked such outrage, and was it justified?

Once again, the opening scenario is as macabre and mysterious as anything in the Holmes canon. Once again, the reader is drawn by the irresistible temptation to discover the answers to a series of extraordinary questions. Why has the notorious Lady Sannox 'absolutely and forever taken the veil' and made it clear that 'the world would see her no more'? Why was her lover, the celebrated operating surgeon Douglas Stone, a 'man of steel nerves', found one morning by his valet, 'seated on one side of his bed, smiling pleasantly upon the universe, with both legs jammed into one side of his breeches and his great brain about as valuable as a cap full of porridge'?

Doyle chose a title much plainer than those of other tales of terror such as 'The Nightmare Room' and 'The Horror of the Heights', as a counterpoint to the lurid plot, but his real focus is not on Lady Sannox, but on Stone. Stone is another Jekyll and Hyde, capable of achieving greatness in any of a dozen lines of life, but 'his vices were as magnificent as his virtues, and infinitely more picturesque.' He is rich but extravagant, sensual and crazed with passion for Lady Sannox, the loveliest woman in London. She is the former Marion Dawson, an actress who met her wealthy but reclusive husband when he indulged his own love of the stage by renting a theatre.

The couple's affair sparks a scandal, but Stone cares nothing for the damage to his reputation. He is about to visit his lover for an evening tryst when a visitor arrives at his consulting room, rather as clients came to 221b Baker Street seeking Holmes' aid. Hamil Ali, from Smyrna, offers Stone one hundred pounds in gold for an hour's work. Greed prompts him to accompany the elderly Turk, although he hesitates when the dreadful nature of his task becomes apparent.

As in Doyle's descriptions of Stoke Moran and Bellingham's room, an exotic context – a room full of 'strange pipes and grotesque weapons', a mysterious poison, a veiled patient drugged with opium – creates an atmosphere brimming with menace. Stone is unwilling to return the money and risk professional embarrassment if, as Hamil Ali fears, the patient dies because surgery to remove poisoned flesh is delayed. The woman is not absolutely unconscious, but Stone agrees to use his knife before the operation causes even greater pain.

What Stone does destroys him, and the woman he adored. Significantly, the knife is a bistoury, a scalpel used for castration, and the lovers suffer a metaphorical castration, victims of the cuckolded husband's cold-blooded ruthlessness. The story is artistically successful not least because Doyle plants clues early to the outcome, playing as fair with his reader as any author of detective fiction. We are told that Lord Sannox is a talented actor, and his strength of purpose hinted at through mention of the way he once broke in a horse.

His scheme succeeds, but the critic from *The Spectator* missed a telling line close to the end of the story: 'But Lord Sannox did not laugh now. Something like fear sharpened and hardened his features.' Doyle conveys that revenge's pleasure will prove illusory with a subtlety all too easy to under-estimate. For all the period flavour of his tales, his mastery of technique sets an example to writers of any era, and is as evident in 'The Case of Lady Sannox' as in any of the justly celebrated stories about Sherlock Holmes.

Ten Essential Stories

'J. Habakuk Jephson's Statement' (1884)
'The Red-Headed League' (1891)★
'The Man with the Twisted Lip' (1891)
'The Speckled Band' (1892)★
'The Copper Beeches' (1892)
'Silver Blaze' (1892)
'Lot No.249' (1892)★
'The Case of Lady Sannox' (1893)★
'The Man with the Watches' (1898)
'The Leather Funnel' (1903)

Frank Cottrell Boyce

on

Anton Chekhov

MY GRANDAD WAS born with a caul. In those days there was a widely held superstition among sailors that anyone born with a caul could never drown. I never met him but I'm guessing that if you were – as he was – a sailor during the War, it was comforting to believe that you weren't going to drown. When he was first married, he jumped ship – running home instead of embarking. He was arrested and thrown into the Bridewell but set free when the news came that his ship had gone down with almost all hands. Maybe he thought that the caul – his luck – had saved him. He got safely through the whole War and was on his way home – just a short swim from Wales – when his ship hit a mine. He was the stoker. His epic, sweaty, hellish job was to keep the fires going. He wasn't supposed to be on duty at the time. He was covering for someone else. He didn't drown when the engines blew. He was boiled alive.

I lived with my grandmother – his wife – when I was small, in a little flat on Stanley Road near the docks in Liverpool. Apart from the odd excursion to the city centre (two stops away), I don't remember her ever straying beyond the little network of streets that was her parish. Yet there was a glass cupboard in the corner of the parlour that was stuffed with the fine, untouchable things that Grandad had brought back from his voyages in the South China Seas or over the Atlantic. A pale tea service so delicate it seemed to tremble like a sea creature behind the glass, a chunk of coral, a shell with Psalm 107 burned into it and a varnished porcupine fish.

That's about all I know about my grandad.

My father barely knew him – he was at sea for most of Dad's childhood and then he was dead. So he didn't talk about him much. My grandma didn't talk about anyone much. So I hardly ever gave my grandad a second thought. One day I was at a film festival doing press for a film I'd written. In the interval between interviews, it looked rude to pick up a book, so I noodled around on my phone and found 'Gusev'. That was the first time I read it. Technologically, sociologically, geographically and emotionally I was a solar system distant from my grandma's flat. But one paragraph in, for the first time in my life, I saw in my imagination, Grandad. Everything about the story lead me to think of him.

Gusev is an orderly heading home to Russia in the sick bay of a tramp steamer. Talkative and feverish, he annoys one of the other passengers – Pavel Ivanitch – by worrying that the ship will be broken on the back of a big fish, or that the wind will 'break its chains'. As he slips in and out of consciousness, he has visions of life at home. Heartbreakingly these visions feature a pond – a domestic manageable version of the sea. Eventually, he dies and his body is sewn up in sailcloth, and tipped overboard. It splashes into the sea and the foam makes it look as though he is wrapped lace. He disappears beneath the waves. Then Chekhov produces his amazing ending, following Gusev's corpse as it sinks to the sea floor, past startled pilot fish and a curious shark.

Part of the reason I had such a strong reaction, of course, is that my grandad is the only near relative I've got whose corpse is rolling around on the bottom of the sea. There's also the fact that Gusev is returning from a war, and that he is dreaming of home, that he didn't belong out there on the sea.

On top of all that though, Gusev just does seem like a real person and this seems like a real incident. This happens so often when you're reading Chekhov – that feeling that you're reading about something that really happened. How does he do this?

To start with, of course, he is often writing about people and places he had really seen and experienced. He was out and about in the world, with his eyes open. In 1890 he spent three months trekking across Siberia to get to the penal colony at Sakhalin. On the way he wrote extraordinary, vivid letters to his sister. He came back on a steamer and there were two passengers on board who were extremely ill. The character of Gusev has the kind of oddity that you feel comes from observation. He dislikes Chinese people intensely and gets into trouble for beating up four of them. When Pavel Ivanitch asks him why he says, 'Oh nothing. They came into the yard so I hit them.' When he is dead, trussed up in the sailcloth, Chekhov describes him with a startling, vivid but undignified phrase. He looks like a carrot or a radish, broad at the top and narrow at the bottom. And of course he dies – what could be more 'real' than that. Chekhov was a doctor. It's a serious matter when a doctor lets a person die, even if that person is fictional.

The landscape too is drawn from observation. In another of the Siberian letters he describes crossing Lake Baikal and looking down into its crystal clear waters. The first time I read it, I felt a shock of delight, thinking Oh! That's where he got that amazing ending for Gusev.

The extraordinary thing about any Chekhov story is that when you begin to read one you have no idea where it's going to end up. You can easily imagine the story that De Maupassant, for instance, would have made of my grandad's life. The Macbethy irony of him believing that just because you couldn't drown you wouldn't die at sea and then – ha ha, cruel fate – he's boiled instead. He should have known! But for me the most arresting thing about his life was how utterly unpredictable its consequences were. If he hadn't jumped ship that night, been prepared to be locked up for an extra night with his wife, I wouldn't be here writing. I wouldn't exist. Nor would my children, my siblings, my cousins. Dozens of people are only alive because of his tipsy whim.

Gusev is unpredictable in the way that life is. It starts with a kind of comedy routine between the ignorant Gusev and the superior Pavel Ivanitch but ends up with that soaring, sacramental prose poem. Writers who try to imitate Chekhov sometimes mistake this unpredictability for randomness, a trudging 'realism' or worse 'honesty'. But Chekhov isn't a journalist or a memoirist. He began as a hack, writing skits and sketches. 'Oh with what trash I began,' he wrote later. He can write anywhere – for instance on a tramp steamer returning from Sakhalin – about anything – for instance a garrulous sick passenger. These are the things that being a hack teaches you. He also has a hack's massive repertoire of tricks and techniques. Chekhov's unpredictability doesn't come from rejecting artifice and contrivance. It comes from being an absolute master of artifice and contrivance. If you go back through the story you will see that that utterly unexpected, hairs-on-the-back-of-your-neck ending, is perfectly set up. In Gusev's silly nonsense about wind and chains and giant fish, in his remembered pond, the sea is always threatening to overwhelm the story. This is true tonally too. Gusev and Pavel Ivanitch are both convincing individual characters – brilliantly observed – but as they bicker, they move further and further apart until each comes to stand for a different view of life. Without you really noticing, a sort of Platonic dialogue emerges, which gathers in urgency as Gusev sails towards his death. Line by line the comedy routine becomes a philosophical debate. There's a mimetic shift. Does life mean anything or not? Does Gusev mean anything or not?

Pavel Ivanitch dismisses Gusev's chances of ever grasping the point of life. 'Foolish, pitiful man,' he says, 'you don't understand anything.' Yet Gusev reaches out for understanding:

> A vague urge disturbs him. He drinks water, but that isn't it. He stretches towards the port-hole and breathes in the hot, dank air, but that isn't it either. He tries to think of home and frost – and it still isn't right. (Chekhov 2008: 51)

Chekhov's great tenderness is that his story seems to be reaching out for a shape and an ending, just as Gusev himself tries to reach out through his fever for a meaning. They're in this together. Gusev can't pin down a meaning for himself but he has a sense that there is one out there somewhere in the complexity of times and tides. Maybe it would all make sense to my grandad if he could see what began that night he jumped ship.

Then there's the ending. In one sense it shows us Gusev as nothing but a piece of meat, dumped over the side, sinking to the bottom. Chekhov once said that his holy of holies was the human body and the end of this story brutally converts Gusev into a physical object – a chunk of protein in the food chain, a piece of meat. But we're also overwhelmed by the sense of the grandeur and beauty of that food chain, of what a magnificent thing meat is. It's impossible to read that section without being pulled up short by how fragile and ridiculous we are – like a carrot or a radish – but also how beautiful – wrapped in lace. It describes life reduced to its components but it also recalls inevitably Psalm 107 – the psalm that was inscribed on my grandad's shell.

> They that go down to the sea in ships, that do business in great waters; these see the works of the Lord, and his wonders in the deep.

Ten Essential Stories

'The Steppe' (1888)
'The Bet' (1889)
'Gusev' (1890)★
'The Grasshopper' (1892)
'Ward 6' (1892)
'Rothschild's Fiddle' (1894)
'About Love' (1898)
'Gooseberries' (1898)
'The Darling' (1899)
'The Lady and the Lapdog' (1899)

Adam Roberts

on

Rudyard Kipling

IT'S HARD BEING an admirer of Kipling when your political sympathies are like mine. Empire; war; women; concepts of duty – a whole ideological globe has swung ponderously around on its axis since his day. Nor were Kipling's ideological beliefs marginal to his work. He really did hero-worship Cecil Rhodes. He really did think women didn't deserve to have the vote. And yet of all English short story writers he is simply the most technically gifted; the one I reread most often, and from whom I have learned the most. Danny Karlin calls him 'one of the three best short story writers in English, along with Henry James and Hemingway, his contemporaries in the golden age of the genre' (Karlin 1999: xvi). That's right, I think, although he has a greater concision of imaginative force than the former and a subtlety of touch of which the latter could only dream.

In what ways, then, is Kipling so good? He does many technical writerly things really well; but then plenty of other good writers can do those things too. By this, I mean things like his genius for visual and physical description and his expressive facility with spoken idioms – not only in dialogue (though his ear for lower-middle-class speech was marvellous) but in his more extended monologue pieces. He evokes the worlds of his stories expertly, with expertly selected telling detail. He puts more characterisation into a figure's mode of speaking than into tabulated accounts of exterior appearance, and more into the *way* each one speaks than what he or she says. He cleaves always to those same Copybook Headings (appropriating, of course, Kipling's own phrase) to which all creative writers must pay attention if they wish to thrive: 'Show, Don't Tell' and 'Less Is More'.

Of course, lots of writers can do this. But there are things that Kipling invented in the short story mode, and of which he is still nonpareil. This has to do with an ability to focus *ambiguity* in order to magnify the emotional impact of the tale. At key moments Kipling finds ways of neither showing *nor* telling in a way that raises the through-force of the whole.

There are two main ways in which he does this, and both are worth the close attention of anybody interested in how to construct the best short fiction. One is that he knows how to hold off our readerly satisfaction. He can, like the Victorians from which he learned his craft, make 'em laugh and make 'em cry, but he brings 'make 'em wait' out of its natural home in the extended prose narrative and applies it to short fiction – a bold but brilliant move. Bold because there is assumed to be a greater imperative in short fiction than elsewhere to hook the reader from the get-go: to crack on with the story, to open with a hook and then bang-bang-bang. Yet most Kipling shorts seem to take a long time to get to the meat of the matter; and it is only when we finish reading that we understand how essential the slow burn is to the effectiveness of the whole. The second way in which he construes ambiguity is by simply *not disclosing* what is at the heart of the tale. I'll come back to that in a minute.

For a masterpiece of narrative postponement we might look at 'The Man Who Would Be King'. At over 14000 words it's long for a short story – novella length, by modern standards. More, the portion of the tale we might be tempted to abstract as 'the story' is much briefer. Most of the story as a whole is given over to (what it would be a mistake to call) 'the frame': a narrator, modelled on the young Kipling, encounters two adventurers, Daniel Dravot and Peachey Carnehan. He renders these men various small assistances, partly because he likes them and partly because they, like he, are Masons. They visit the narrator in the newspaper office where he works, consult reference books and maps, and tell him they plan to become kings of Kafiristan, to the north of India. By the story's halfway point, this is all that has happened; everything is oriented proleptically, looking forward to a story that has yet to be told. It is an exciting story: when John Huston made a movie of the story in 1975, starring Sean Connery and Michael Caine ('Adventure in all its glory!' shouted the film posters) he didn't drop the frame entirely, but he did shrink it greatly, and put the events of Carenhan's narrative front and centre. Kipling does the opposite. He withholds and postpones, because he knows that what the reader is *not* told intrigues her far more than what is laid out for her.

So, the paragraph immediately before the two adventurers arrive in the narrator's office is a tour de force of this kind of writing: evoking the oppressive heat of an Indian night with some vividly pitched description, but doing nothing more by way of moving the story on than intimating that *something is about to happen* – and not even giving us a clue as to what that 'something' might be. All we know is that the newspaper has had to delay going to press, waiting on some news (a dying king, a popular uprising) that may or may not be telegraphed over from Europe.

> It was a pitchy black night, as stifling as a June night can be, and the *loo*, the red-hot wind from the westward, was booming among the tinder-dry trees and pretending that the rain was on its heels. Now and again a spot of almost boiling water would fall on the dust with the flop of a frog, but all our weary world

knew that was only pretence. It was a shade cooler in the press-room than the office, so I sat there, while the type ticked and clicked, and the night-jars hooted at the windows, and the all but naked compositors wiped the sweat from their foreheads and called for water. The thing that was keeping us back, whatever it was, would not come off, though the *loo* dropped and the last type was set, and the whole round earth stood still in the choking heat, with its finger on its lip, to wait the event. I drowsed, and wondered whether the telegraph was a blessing, and whether this dying man, or struggling people, was aware of the inconvenience the delay was causing. There was no special reason beyond the heat and worry to make tension, but, as the clock-hands crept up to three o'clock and the machines spun their fly-wheels two and three times to see that all was in order, before I said the word that would set them off, I could have shrieked aloud. (Karlin 1999: 62–63)

Kipling's use of detail – the occasional spots of 'boiling' rain that fall on the dust 'with the flop of a frog' is especially brilliant – is the kind of thing that makes a fellow writer want to stand up and applaud. He drops in Indian words sparingly, but to pinpoint estranging effect. Above all, he keeps his reader poised, and pumps up the tension.

Carnehan and Dravot, when they turn up, are big men ('we have decided,' they say, 'that India isn't big enough for such as us'). This is how the narrator conveys their heft:

They certainly were too big for the office. Dravot's beard seemed to fill half the room and Carnehan's shoulders the other half, as they sat on the big table. (Karlin 1999: 64)

The size of the table somehow transfers itself to our sense of the physical bulk of the characters; and reducing the pair only to a beard and a pair of shoulders much more effectively evokes the two men's size in the reader's mind than more detailed or plodding itemisations of the complete thing could.

The second half of the story contains Carnehan's inset narrative, when he returns to the newspaper offices 'two years later': a broken man. And it satisfyingly pays off the promise the first half made as regards exciting narrative; but what makes it really stand out is its creation of a particular voice. Carnehan is not educated; and his idiom reflects this – he says 'mountaineous' rather than mountainous, and certain words are rendered in cod-Dickensian cockney ('tremenjus', 'impidence'). Kipling was fond of ventriloquizing working class idiolects, in his verse as well as his prose, and on occasion it makes the reading hard work. 'The Bonds of Discipline' (1904) is a fine story, but hiking through the thicket of apostrophe-pruned words and cockney naval idiom can be hard work – "an' 'ummin' to 'imself. Our cook 'ated 'ummin' [...] "Boots in the galley," 'e says. "Cook's mate, cast out an' abolish this cutter–cuddlin' aborigine's boots!" They was 'ove overboard in quick time, an' that was what 'Op was lyin' to for'." There are passages in *that* story, I confess, I can only comprehend by reading aloud – though, as the story is about a deliberate attempt to mislead and bamboozle a man's comprehension, perhaps that's only fitting. As a general rule a writer *is* well advised to steer clear of dialect orthography – but Carnehan's narrative in 'The Man Who Would Be King' is an object lesson in how to do it well. The whole is not only readily comprehensible, moving its narrative briskly along; using a speaker of Carnehan's background and outlook enables Kipling to achieve effects of sudden eloquence and poetic vividness that a more conventional style of narration simply could not effect. It reads as both natural and powerful when (for instance) Carnehan recalls sitting around the campfire with Dravot:

'Dravot used to make us laugh in the evenings when all the people was cooking their dinners – cooking their dinners, and [...] what did they do then? They lit little fires with sparks that went into Dravot's beard, and we all laughed – fit to die. Little red fires they was, going into Dravot's big red beard – so funny.' His eyes left mine and he smiled foolishly. (Karlin 1999: 70)

Kipling is careful with his use of colour: here the red of Dravot's beard, and his fiery, martial temper, are epitomised in one vivid visual image; later the gold of his crown is described as 'red' too, as is the blood spilt in the final uprising. When Carnehan returns, a broken man, he is described as drained of colour: 'his drawn face, surmounted by a shock of grey hair', crawling in 'the white dust of the roadside'; but the last thing we hear him say is when he sings an old hymn:

'The Son of Man goes forth to war,
A golden crown to gain;
His blood-red banner streams afar –
Who follows in his train?' (Karlin 1999: 86)

These colours are effective means of evoking the particularity of a scene in a reader's mind, but they can do more than that. Here, unfussily but effectively, Kipling patterns-out the larger themes of his tale: war and glory, pain and defeat.

'They', one of Kipling's most moving stories, achieves its emotional impact by taking the principle of 'less is more' to a sort of extreme. It is a ghost story in which not only is the word 'ghost' never used, but the very concept of *ghosts* is never alluded to. And this is exactly the right way of proceeding, of course; because that's what ghosts are – not spectral *presences* so much as a kind of emotional and physical *absence*. As a story, 'They' depends upon a kind of cumulative narrative innuendo: our suspicion that there is something strange about the children in the house builds; we learn of the old blind woman's 'special' sight; of the local villager's euphemism for children who have died ('walking in the woods'); of the fact that both the butler and the narrator have been bereaved of their own children. But as much of the short story is concerned with (expert and evocative) descriptions of the landscape of southern England.

The one stylistic risk Kipling takes comes near the end, when the narrator responds to the old woman's statement that she has never had children with '"Be very glad then," said I, for my soul was torn open within me.' Those last eight words might, in a different context, come over as merely melodramatic, or worse as bathetic. In this case they don't, because they are the only direct reference in the whole story to the overwhelming emotions generated by the narrator's encounter with the children. What is not said is infinitely more powerful than what is. The moment when the narrator finally understands that he has been dealing not with coy or playful children but with their shades is, in keeping with the whole story, obliquely put:

> I felt my relaxed hand taken and turned softly between the soft hands of a child. So at last I had triumphed. In a moment I would turn and acquaint myself with those quick-footed wanderers...
>
> The little brushing kiss fell in the centre of my palm – as a gift on which the fingers were, once, expected to close: as the all faithful half-reproachful signal of a waiting child not used to neglect even when grown-ups were busiest – a fragment of the mute code devised very long ago.
>
> Then I knew. And it was as though I had known from the first day. (Karlin 1999: 273)

Another writer might spell-out more directly that the narrator is here recognising the kiss as that his own dead child had used to give him. By not saying this – by instead characterising the moment of contact and revelation in terms of 'mute code' – Kipling magnifies the affective impact enormously. The mode of telling in this story is that of *missing something* – precisely because the world of the story is missing something: the children themselves. They exist at the margins, hiding amongst the trees, elusive, because that's how the dead exist for those of us they leave behind. Kipling captures the depth of the uniquely ghastly sorrow caused by the death of a child by writing about how it cannot be squarely faced.

It sometimes seems to me that there is nothing about sadness and loss Kipling doesn't understand. And by the same token, he understands anger in a way profounder than almost any other writer. This is, in part, because he was just English enough to comprehend that polite repression of anger works, as muscles down upon the hinges of the skeleton, to articulate anger much more potently than the straightforward venting of one's rage – but not so English as to be persuaded that that was in any sense a good thing. A story like 'How the Rhinoceros Got His Skin', from his once-popular collection of fantastical children's fables *Just So Stories* (1902), treats its subject with whimsical amusement, some of which communicates itself to even the twenty-first century reader. But I've always felt there's a tinge of nightmare about the tale. Certainly the Rhino is impolite, and shouldn't have taken the Parsee's cake; but the punishment it receives, an eternal itching sensation underneath his skin, which, however much he tries, Lady Macbeth-like, to scratch away, will never go away. The Rhino looks the way he does because his own ill-temper, involuted upon his own body, has literally deformed him.

Rage is also at the heart of 'Mary Postgate' (1915), one of the most marvellously chilling stories ever written. It is as clear an example as any in Kipling's oeuvre of his textual strategy of representing something – in this case, the sort of anger that moves human beings to kill – by, as it were, sketching *around* the object: describing everything about its title character *except* her anger. She is, as her reference quoted in the first paragraph says, 'thoroughly conscientious, tidy, companionable, and ladylike.' The very unlikeliness of such

Achillean fury residing in the primly buttoned-down and respectable breast of this governess powers the tale.

> Mary was not young, and though her speech was as colourless as her eyes or her hair, she was never shocked. She listened unflinchingly to every one; said at the end, 'How interesting!' or 'How shocking!' as the case might be, and never again referred to it, for she prided herself on a trained mind, which 'did not dwell on these things.' She was, too, a treasure at domestic accounts, for which the village tradesmen, with their weekly books, loved her not. Otherwise she had no enemies; provoked no jealousy even among the plainest; neither gossip nor slander had ever been traced to her. (Karlin 1999: 337)

This neutrally descriptive style is effective in characterising her as, precisely, colourless; but Kipling is cleverer by also giving us the more caricatured (if affectionately so) way 'Young Wyndham Fowler' sees her: 'calling her "Gatepost," "Postey," or "Packthread," by thumping her between her narrow shoulders, or by chasing her bleating, round the garden, her large mouth open, her large nose high in air, at a stiff-necked shamble very like a camel's.'

The First World War, and Fowler's joining the Flying Corps, is emblematised by the 'cardigan waistcoat' Postgate knits him; and the conversation between Mary and old Miss Fowler – which, incidentally and pleasingly, passes the so-called Bechdel Test – reinforces that her identity exists only in relation to others, in her work as a 'companion'. As ever, Kipling does not *tell* us of her inner yearning, but externalises it in a poetic image, as Wyndham flies his plane over the house.

> For two mornings (he had warned her by postcard) Mary heard the thresh of his propellers at dawn. The second time she ran to the window, and stared at the

whitening sky. A little blur passed overhead. She lifted
her lean arms towards it. (Karlin 1999: 340)

'Lean' is a beautifully judged modifier, there. And without
pause the story runs smoothly on to –

> That evening at six o'clock there came an announcement
> in an official envelope that Second Lieutenant W. Fowler
> had been killed during a trial flight. Death was
> instantaneous. She read it and carried it to Miss Fowler.
> 'I never expected anything else,' said Miss Fowler;
> 'but I'm sorry it happened before he had done
> anything.'
> The room was whirling round Mary Postgate, but
> she found herself quite steady in the midst of it.
> 'Yes,' she said. 'It's a great pity he didn't die in action
> after he had killed somebody.' (Karlin 1999: 341)

The emotional restraint here is at once very English and rather
monstrous. 'But why can't we cry, Mary?' asks Miss Fowler.
'There's nothing to cry for,' is Mary's view. Her wish that
Wyndham had died only *after* killing somebody else intimates,
with clever understatement, that Mary does possess human
grief and anger, but, unable to express it in any conventional
manner, is striving to transfer it onto some other object.

The incinerator, favoured by tidy Miss Fowler and tidier
Mary as a means of completely disposing of waste is deployed
as another piece of psychological externalisation. When Mary
encounters the wounded foreign airman, it is to the incinerator
that she goes:

> 'Laty! Laty! Laty!' [the airman] muttered, while his
> hands picked at the dead wet leaves. There was no doubt
> as to his nationality. It made her so angry that she strode
> back to the destructor, though it was still too hot to use
> the poker there. (Karlin 1999: 347)

The fierce, quasi-erotic joy Mary takes in this young man's death remains extraordinarily startling, even today. A whole Victorian-Edwardian ethos, epitomised by all the clutter of books and clothes that are burnt up in the incinerator, is gifted a sudden release. Mary assumes the pilot is German. He himself begs for a doctor in French – either because he is a German pilot who mistakenly believes he has crashed in France, or because (the more ironic possibility) that he is a *French* aviator who has been assisting the RFC in training its pilots – the British did avail themselves of the superior expertise of the French in this matter in the very early years of the War. The story refuses to resolve this crucial ambiguity; any more than it tells us for sure whether nine-year-old Edna died because an old wall collapsed, or because a bomb was dropped on her. As ever with Kipling, the external data matter much less than the internal ones. 'Mary Postgate' uses its exquisite narrative and descriptive restraint to dramatise the way (as Freud puts it) the repressed not only returns but returns in force.

In some of Kipling's stories the strategic obliqueness of crucial salient details creates a sense of mystery so deep readers are still trying to untangle it. 'Mrs Bathurst' (1904) is a case in point: one of Kipling's most brilliant stories – an involving yet in crucial ways *baffling* portrait of the centripetal forces that work upon the people whose occupations carry them across and back and across again a wide-spaced empire. Kipling evokes the disparateness of this world in the first few paragraphs of the story by piling up place names (Simon's Bay; Glengariff; a seven-coloured sea; Elsie's Peak; hills of False Bay; Buluwayo; Belmont; Tristan D'Acunha; 'Muizenburg, St. James's, and Kalk Bay', Vancouver, Nyassa, Aukland, Mozambique) and peoples (English, the Greeks 'who sell all things at a price', Malays, Indians). The story hops between different speakers, piecing together disparate episodes and slowly bringing into focus its central image: Mrs Bathurst herself. That she never quite comes into focus leaves us with a sense not of frustration or authorial failure, but on the contrary: it leaves us with a sense of a profounder kind of mystery. The conversation between Hooper, Pyecroft and Pritchard is as much about the difficulty of communication itself, as it is about what made Mrs Bathurst so special that Vickery deserted and went on the run just to be with her (if that's what he did):

> 'I don't *see* her yet somehow,' said Hooper, but with sympathy.
> 'She – she never scrupled to feed a lame duck or set 'er foot on a scorpion at any time of 'er life,' Pritchard added valiantly.
> 'That don't help me either. My mother's like that for one.'
> The giant heaved inside his uniform and rolled his eyes at the car-roof. (Karlin 1999: 284)

The challenge Kipling has set himself is to portray what we would nowadays call an 'It-girl'; and he goes about it in a manner both counter-intuitive and brilliantly penetrating.

> 'Then the Western Mail came in to Paddin'ton on the big magic lantern sheet. First we saw the platform empty an' the porters standin' by. Then the engine come in, head on, an' the women in the front row jumped: she headed so straight. Then the doors opened and the passengers came out and the porters got the luggage – just like life. Only – only when any one came down too far towards us that was watchin', they walked right out o' the picture, so to speak. I was 'ighly interested, I can tell you. So were all of us. I watched an old man with a rug 'oo'd dropped a book an' was tryin' to pick it up, when quite slowly, from be'ind two porters – carryin' a little reticule an' lookin' from side to side – comes out Mrs. Bathurst. There was no mistakin' the walk in a hundred thousand. She come forward – right forward – she looked out straight at us

with that blindish look which Pritch alluded to. She
walked on and on till she melted out of the picture –
like – like a shadow jumpin' over a candle, an' as she
went I 'eard Dawson in the ticky seats be'ind sing out:
"Christ! There's Mrs. B.!'" (Karlin 1999: 286-7)

The way Mrs Bathurst is captured, inadvertently, on film (a
piece of film Vickery drags Pyecroft to see over and again) is
canny – because of course film construes sexual desire to this
day in a way real-life can rarely match; but cannier still is
making the obscure object of Vickery's desire *not* a film star
or model, but a widow who runs a hostel for sailors. She is
not remarkable in any way except her unremarkableness, and
in the effect she has on men.

Kipling deliberately withholds the information we need
to 'solve' the story. Why had Mrs Bathurst travelled to Britain?
Was she searching for Vickery, or for another man, or was it
for some other purpose entirely? Who *is* the second figure
burned to 'charcoal' in the teak forest? Vickery's corpse is
identified by his false teeth, but is the other Mrs Bathurst? Is
it even a woman? We may speculate upon these details, and
many have; but we have neither the obligation nor, in fact, the
means actually to resolve them. This is because Kipling's
purpose is not to lay out all the salient details in readily
digestible order but on the contrary to throw our attention
back onto the logic of storytelling itself. The key thing about
a story, he is saying, is not what it is *about* so much as what it
is. The social interaction of it; the quiddity and uniqueness of
its shape and expression; the way character and emotional
force more often emerge through its seams than through
direct presentation. And that is a lesson any writer can usefully
take to heart.

Ten Essential Stories

'The Man Who Would Be King' (1888)★
'The Mary Gloster' (1896)
'How the Rhinoceros Got His Skin' (1902)★
'The Bonds of Discipline' (1903)
'They' (1904)★
'Mrs Bathurst' (1904)★
'In the Presence' (1912)
'Mary Postgate' (1915)★
'Sea Constables' (1915)
'The Bull That Thought' (1924)

Stephen Baxter

on

H.G. Wells

'THE STAR', FIRST published in 1897 by a still-young H.G. Wells, is an account of global disaster compressed into a few thousand words. Startling, terrifying, replete with lovely phrases – and with millions of souls wiped out in a sentence – it is a wonderfully efficient shot of disaster porn.

As a young reader I found the story frustrating; it read more like a compressed novel, or even a movie outline, than a short story, and it left me longing to know more. Now it feels like reading the Book of Revelation on Twitter. Yet the story has always stayed in my mind, and has no doubt influenced me considerably, as a number of my own works show, such as my novel, *Flood* (2008).

More than a century after its first publication, the story has proved to have had an influence far outweighing its few thousand words' length. Following a discussion of the story's sources and techniques, I will argue that in fact one day 'The Star' may come to be regarded as the little story that helped save the world.

'The Star' opens on the first of January, a new year and perhaps the dawn of a new century, with the discovery by an astronomer, Ogilvy, of perturbations of the planet Neptune, caused by the approach to the solar system of a 'strange wanderer' (Wells 2000: 281). The news of this rather abstract event is released to a world 'the greater portion of whose inhabitants were unaware of the existence of the planet Neptune,' (281) and causes no great stir – until the third day of the event, when at dawn in London, there is a blazing light in the sky: 'the yawning policeman saw the thing, the busy crowds in the markets stopped agape.' (282). This spectacle is the result of the collision of the intruding body with Neptune; the resulting incandescent mass is now falling into the heart of the solar system.

A 'master mathematician' calculates the orbit, and is the first to realise that after a deflection by Jupiter the new star will fall directly towards the Earth. The news of this game of cosmic billiards, 'telegraphed all over the world' (283) causes a flight to the churches – but 'nine human beings out of ten were still busy at their common occupations [...] common sense was sturdy everywhere.' (286)

Five days after the Jupiter encounter, the damage begins. The heat of the new star causes thaws and floods; there are earthquakes and volcanoes, and 'a wall of water, fifty feet high, roaring hungrily, [fell] upon the long coasts of Asia, and swept inland across the plains of China' (287). Amid global devastation, there is a remarkable astronomical conjunction as Sun, Moon and star swim together in the same part of the sky – and the star begins to recede: 'The whole land seemed a-wailing, and suddenly there swept a shadow across that furnace of despair, and a breath of cold wind, and a gathering of clouds, out of the cooling air' (288). A diminished mankind is left to explore a changed Earth, 'the sun larger, and the Moon, shrunk to a third of its former size.' (288)

In the final paragraph we see the viewpoint of Martian astronomers who, looking from afar, are astonished 'what a little damage the Earth, which it missed so narrowly, has sustained.' (289)

As a side comment, since Wells' time we have come to a better understanding of the science behind 'The Star': that is, the likely reality that stars might approach each other. Stars do move relative to each other, as they swim in their orbits around the centre of the Galaxy, and some will indeed approach our sun (for one study, see Matthews: 1-9). Proxima Centauri is currently the nearest star to the Sun. In 1946, the year of Wells' death, a Russian astronomer called Vyssotsky noticed that a star known by catalogue number Gliese 710, currently about 63 light years away, seems to be heading straight for us. Recent studies have determined that Gliese 710 will come to within a light year in about 1.3 million years. If a star were to come swimming into the solar system, the effects could well be as Wells sketched, with exceptional tides, geological disruption, tsunamis, and the perturbation of planetary orbits.

Wells, however, knew nothing of this. What, then, were the influences behind the story?

A key motivation for writing the story was simply money. When 'The Star' was first published Wells was 31 years old, and only two years into his career as a professional writer. Although *The Time Machine* (1895) and other early novels had been significant successes, Wells, who had come from a modest background, was already married and was trying to build a career. In an introduction to a 1950s collection of his works, his son Frank would write, 'These stories were written during the few years from 1894. They were written by a professional earning a living. They were written by an exuberantly creative mind and by the shadow of an empty till' (quoted in Foot: 27). Hastily written commercial ventures these early stories may have been, but they pioneered ideas that would underpin the genre of science fiction to this day – even though the generic name itself would not be coined for another quarter-century.

In the process of turning out these stories, Wells sought ideas wherever he could find them, from his reading of fiction, from factual knowledge – and, as his career developed, as spin-offs from his own growing body of work.

There were fictional precedents for tales of close encounters with cosmic objects, such as Jules Verne's *Hector Servadac*, in which a comet brushes the Earth and flies off with a few chunks of it. We know Wells read Jules Verne.

More specifically, Aldiss and others have noted (Aldiss & Wingrive, p454 n8), 'striking similarities' between Wells' story and Camille Flammarion's *La Fin du Monde* (aka *Omega: The Last Days of the World*) (1893) in which a cometary collision appears likely to destroy the world altogether. Flammarion (1842-1925) was an astronomer, a pioneering populariser of science, and a writer of scientific romances that dramatised the grand cosmological ideas his profession was developing. *Omega* opens in the twenty-fifty century, when an astronomer in Asia detects a comet *en route* for an apparent collision with the Earth. This is extensively debated in Paris, a hub of a United States of Europe. In the end the Earth passes through the distended gaseous body of the comet; there are spectacular light shows, heating and gaseous effects in the atmosphere, and some (relatively) minor impacts with cometary fragments. Casualties are light, and the Earth and humanity pass on, serene.

How much influence can we detect of this book on Wells? Surely there is some. But the incoming menace is not a 'star' as in Wells' story but a comet, an object from within the solar system; the scale is altogether different. And the nature of the 'impact' as depicted is entirely different too. Flammarion's cometary shaking-up of mankind actually seems a clearer influence on Wells' later novel *In the Days of the Comet* (1906).

More significantly, *Omega* is rather inferior fiction. Much of the text consists of professors expounding on aspects of the coming disaster. There's none of the human perspective we see in 'The Star': '"What is a new star to me?" cried the weeping woman, kneeling beside her dead' (283). There is more artistry in that one sentence of Wells' than in all of Flammarion.

Flammarion is indeed a likely influence on Wells, but 'The Star' is a sufficiently successful and distinctive piece of fiction to stand as thoroughly original.

Wells' key inspiration for the story was probably his own scientific understanding, as nurtured in his years as a student teacher of science at the Normal School of Science, later Imperial College, London, where he studied evolution, chemistry, astronomy and other subjects. In the story's opening paragraphs Wells shows he is well read in interstellar geography: 'Few people without a training in science can realise the huge isolation of the solar system...' (280). The nearest star, he says, is at least 'twenty million times a million miles' away – the best part of four light years, which is close to the modern estimate, first established by an astronomer called Thomas Henderson in the 1830s.

And Wells would surely have been aware of well-established evidence that large masses can perturb planetary orbits. Indeed the discovery of planet Neptune in 1846 was a famous consequence of the analysis by British and French scholars of that planet's gravitational perturbations of the orbit of Uranus, the next planet in. In 1897, such spectacular discoveries would have been as current in the public mind as, say, the discovery of the DNA double helix is today. Perhaps the story's opening with the star's deflection at Neptune is an echo of this source.

Finally, a key source of ideas for any experienced writer is as spin-offs from his or her own other projects. In 1897 Wells' mind would have been full of relevant material for a story like 'The Star' through his work on *The War of the Worlds*, an epic novel of Martian invasion, first published in the same year. There are thematic links between story and novel – both are tales of cosmic intervention, without mind in the case of 'The Star', with conscious intent in the case of *The War of the Worlds*. Specific links include cameos in both works by an astronomer called 'Ogilvy', and the reference to Martian astronomers at the close of the story. Perhaps creatively 'The Star' is most usefully seen as a by-product of the swirl of ideas that went into the creation of *The War of the Worlds* – or even a sketch of an alternate version of that novel, if Wells had not hit on the idea of writing a parable of imperial invasion in conversation with his brother Frank (to whom *The War of the Worlds* is dedicated).

There is also of course a wider background to works of apocalypse and catastrophe, like Wells' novel and story. Western culture has a deep-rooted expectation of apocalypse just around the corner that seems to date back as far as the Book of Revelation (Pearson). Arguably the most influential book ever written, Revelation's picture of the coming last days, when all will be swept aside in a time of disaster and battles before the coming of a new order, remains a template for our many views of the apocalyptic future.

Certainly this sort of pattern is discernible in many of Wells' tales of disasters such as *The War of the Worlds* and *In the Days of the Comet*. Even in 'The Star' Wells finds room to hint of a new order to come once the star has passed: 'But of the new brotherhood that grew presently among men, of the saving of laws and books and machines, of the strange change that had come over Iceland and Greenland and the shores of Baffin's Bay, so that the sailors coming there presently found them green and gracious, and could scarce believe their eyes, this story does not tell.' (289)

Wells, however, had rejected religion, and there is no sense of a divine judgement behind the catastrophe of 'The Star'. On the contrary the sense is of random destruction: 'It would seem, gentlemen, if I may put the thing clearly and briefly, that – Man has lived in vain.' (284)

To tell his story, an epic compressed into a few pages, Wells uses almost cinematic techniques: as a young man he was impressed by the imaginative possibilities of early cinema. To depict a global disaster Wells uses a global scatter of viewpoints, sketched in the briefest of phrases: 'All over the dusky quickening country it could be seen – and out at sea by seamen watching for the day – a great white star, come suddenly into the westward sky!' (282)

As in others of Wells' early works, there are no real characters in the story. The only developed figure is a 'master mathematician' who computes the orbit of the star and predicts doomsday. Mostly Wells sticks to a lofty omniscient viewpoint, as if filmed from orbit: 'For a space the star... showed with pitiless brilliance the wide and populous country [of China]; towns and villages with their pagodas and trees, roads, wide cultivated fields, millions of sleepless people staring in helpless terror at the incandescent sky...' (287). This is a godlike viewpoint, capable of zooming out even as far as Mars in the final paragraphs – and yet Wells shows the value of zooming *in* briefly, such as on 'the weeping woman, kneeling beside her dead.'

Even the master mathematician is a type rather than a person, to be compared with other unnamed figures in Wells' early novels such as the Time Traveller of *The Time Machine* or the Artilleryman of *The War of the Worlds*. In a sense this lack of characterisation shows 'The Star' to be a quintessential science fiction story, in which the driving force is the idea in relation to humanity. 'The Star' is vivid, human and unforgettable, but it is not shown on a human *scale*; it is not a character study, unless the suffering Earth itself is considered as a character.

Another key story-telling technique used in all good disaster stories is a countdown to doom – which depends, of course, on having a character available who is aware that peril is approaching, and can derive a timetable for it. In 'The Star' this is the 'master mathematician': 'He looked at it as one might look into the eyes of a brave enemy. "You may kill me," he said after a silence. "But I can hold you – and all the universe for that matter – in the grip of this small brain. I would not change. Even now."' (284)

The lasting influences of the story derive from its theme, of a mindless apocalypse, and the techniques Wells used.

Consider the very 'Star'-like *When Worlds Collide*, best known as the 1951 movie directed by Rudolph Mate and produced by George Pal, but based on a novel published in 1933 by Philip Wylie and Edwin Balmer. In the movie cosmic intruders once more sail into the solar system, not one object this time but two: a sun with an Earthlike planet (Bellos and Xyra). Earth is doomed – but, unlike Wells' scenario, mankind is saved as a handful of people cross to the wandering planet in an 'ark' spacecraft.

In the movie, although the character stories are stronger, just as in Wells' story we are shown worldwide viewpoints, multiple scenes of people praying in Rome and Mecca, cities burning, forests burning, tidal waves – and there are eerie post-disaster views too, of ships dumped between city skyscrapers. As for a countdown clock, the movie's 'master mathematician' is a clattering Differential Analyser, a 1950s Meccano-like mechanical computer – and the countdown itself is portrayed by the simple, unforgettable device of a tearaway calendar.

Was *When Worlds Collide* inspired by 'The Star'? There was no formal credit, but Arthur C. Clarke, who reviewed the movie (not very positively) when it first appeared certainly thought so (Clarke, p. 108). One of the novel's authors, Philip Wylie (1902-71), a successful commercial author, was very aware of Wells' work; he wrote screenplays for movie versions of *The Island of Doctor Moreau* (as *The Island of Lost Souls*, 1932) and *The Invisible Man* (1933). Circumstantially it seems highly likely that 'The Star' was a key source. The movie itself was certainly influential. In 1993 Clute and Nicholls described this movie as 'helping to spark the 1950s sf-movie boom'.

The story also had a lasting influence on science fiction itself. When his first masterpiece *Last and First Men* was first published in 1931, Olaf Stapledon wrote to Wells: 'My debt to you is too large and I was not properly aware of it... A man does not record his debt to the air he breathes in common with everyone else.' And in this letter he specifically acknowledged the influence of 'The Star' and *The War of the Worlds* (Stapledon to Wells, October 1931, quoted in Smith 1986). Much of Stapledon's work concerned the interaction of the human with the cosmic, as expressed in the fictions of Wells he cited. The lofty omniscient perspective Wells used in 'The Star' characterised Stapledon's great book, and episodes of cosmic catastrophe reminiscent of 'The Star' might include the desperate flight of the 'Eighth Men' from the swelling-up of the Sun (Chapter XIII), in a sub-chapter Stapledon called, with Martian aloofness, 'A Minor Astronomical Event'.

A still more significant reference to Wells' story came a few decades later. In Arthur C. Clarke's *Rendezvous with Rama* (1973), an astronomer detects an object called Rama approaching the solar system. 'Perhaps Rama was a dead sun... There flashed briefly through Dr Stenton's mind the memory of that timeless classic, H.G. Wells' "The Star"... Across two centuries of time it had lost none of its magic and terror. He would never forget the images of hurricanes and tidal waves, of cities sliding into the sea...' (Chapter 2). In this case Rama turns out to be a spacecraft, a much smaller object, and a drama of exploration and alien contact unfolds.

The longer-term significance of Clarke's reference comes from the reason Stenton was looking for wandering objects in the first place. In an almost throwaway opening chapter Clarke shows how an asteroid impact on Venice leads to setting up of a detect-and-deflect programme called Spaceguard: 'There would be no next time' (*Rendezvous,* Chapter 1).

Unlike the approach of a rogue star, which as we have seen is a remote threat, astronomers became aware throughout the twentieth century of the very real danger of impacts from comets and asteroids. In 1980, Alvarez *et al* demonstrated from relic traces that the extinction event that destroyed the dinosaurs was caused by a tremendous impact (*Science*: 1085-1108). This mounting awareness culminated in attempts to establish a real–world 'Spaceguard'. After a near–miss by an asteroid in 1989, Congress ordered NASA to conduct a survey to improve the detection rate of threatening asteroids, and to consider ways of deflecting them. Such studies have continued to this day.

The significance for our discussion here is that it seems to have been Clarke's outlining in *Rama* of the threat and the possibility of defence, and in particular his coining of the word 'Spaceguard', that focussed minds enough to create these initiatives. And since 'The Star' was so clearly one source of inspiration for *Rama*, if it ever turns out that Earth is saved by some descendant of Spaceguard, we will remember Wells' story as one link in the chain of conceptualisation and actualisation that rescued mankind: the little story that saved the world.

With its influence on modern science fiction, on the disaster–fiction sub–genre, and on real–world attempts to handle asteroid threats, just as the few thousand words of 'The Star' strain to contain the epochal events it describes, so Wells' story's influence on its genre and on the real world belies its brevity.

Ten Essential Stories

'In the Abyss' (1896)
'The Star' (1897)★
'The Crystal Egg' (1897)
'The Man Who Could Work Miracles' (1898)
'A Story of the Days to Come' (1899)
'The Land Ironclads' (1903)
'The Country of the Blind' (1904)
'The Empire of the Ants' (1905)
'The Door in the Wall' (1906)
'The Grisly Folk' (1921)

Stuart Evers

on

Sherwood Anderson

IN THE FINAL room of a recent George Bellows exhibition at the Royal Academy – the walls hanging with vast, Vermeer-inspired portraits – a placard explained the events leading to the artist's death. Its last sentences were taken from a piece written by Sherwood Anderson. Bellows' paintings 'keep telling you things,' it said. 'They are telling you that George Bellows died too young. They are telling you that he was after something, that he was always after it.' Ignoring the paintings, I read that last sentence again. And then again. And then again.

It's a sentence that is perfectly, piercingly Anderson: melancholic yet enigmatic; elegiac, yet ambivalent. It is part of a eulogy that poses as many questions as it answers. What are the 'things' these paintings tell us? Is there ever a death that doesn't occur 'too young'? And most pertinently, what was Bellows 'after' with such vigour?

I read that sentence and wondered whether there was a slyness to it, an underlying suggestion that Bellows was a striving artist, but one who had never found his true direction. And on reading it again, I was struck by how this same muted panegyric could be applied to many of the characters Anderson created in his short fiction. Those men and women who are always after something, but rarely, if ever, find it. Characters who, in their stories of alienation, broken dreams

79

and self-deception are the precursors to and inspirations for, some of the finest American writing of the Twentieth Century.

And this is where Sherwood Anderson's reputation now largely sits: as an influencer of others, a lamplighter for later innovations. His stories reach back into oral storytelling modes – conversational, barflyish, gossipy – but are closely allied to the themes and concerns of an America growing into its new century. These are tales of ordinary people, living ordinary lives, in ordinary towns. And yet in each of these lives there is the undertow of tragedy, of something left unfulfilled, of a life lacking 'adventure', or of something dark in the soul. Anderson honed these tropes and gave them a uniquely American flavour. Faulkner, Hemingway and Steinbeck were the most famous of his early disciples, but there is something of Anderson that remains in the great American short story writers who followed – Grace Paley, Raymond Carver, Flannery O'Connor, Richard Yates, Eudora Welty. He's there, ghosting about in their writerly DNA, but there's more to reading Anderson than just going to the source.

An author's influence should always be separated from his or her quality as a writer. Reading *Winesburg, Ohio* is not enhanced by knowing Faulkner was energised by Anderson's prose, it can only be judged by reading the stories. Stories that remain fresh and vital, stories that wrestle with the same tics and foibles of contemporary life as we do a century later. Stories that resonate, yet are very much of their time. Stories that appear conventional, yet pull apart at the seams of what a story can and should be. Stories that get under the skin of characters and place with dexterity and compression. Stories that look effortless on the surface, but are riven and hewn with deft, subtle artistry.

In a specialized reading list for his 1977 course at the Naropa Institute – 'The Literary History of the Beat Generation' – Allen Ginsberg chose amongst a mammoth accumulation of texts, 'Hands' a story from *Winesburg, Ohio*. Alongside the radicals, the drunks, the mystics and the friends of Ginsberg, Sherwood Anderson – a surveyor of small-town life, a 'conventional' writer, a dealer in realism, even of nostalgia, of whimsy – seems oddly nestled on the same list as Andre Gide and Gregory Corso and Jean Genet. But in content, in execution and in subject matter, 'Hands' is as revolutionary, as ludic, and as dark in its restraint, implications and suggestions, as the Beats were in their explicitness.

It is tempting to go through 'Hands' line by line, sentence by sentence. Not for their beauty so much – though there is clearly beauty there – but to trace and analyse the way Anderson switches pace, changes tack, offers information, holds it back, clears his throat, backtracks, repeats himself. To do so would take far longer than the two and half thousand words of the story. To do so might also be to take away some of its hayseed-ish magic. But to understand how Anderson constructs his stories, how he generates atmosphere and emotional connection, it is at sentence level that any examination must start. Take the opening line:

> Upon the half decayed veranda of a small frame house that stood near the edge of a ravine near the town of Winesburg, Ohio, a fat little old man walked nervously up and down. (Anderson 1992: 27)

This is a distillation of the story's themes and concerns: one sentence that rhythmically builds to create a sense of someone caught between two very distinct worlds. In the first place, the veranda is only half rotted, a house therefore neither old nor new. The house abuts both the civility and community of the town and the danger and oblivion of the ravine. Between the two is a fat little old man – the image of avuncular safety and calm – but he is fretting and pacing up and down the boards. This is someone awash in oppositions.

There are further oppositions as the paragraph continues. A field that was sown for crop is overgrown with nothing more than mustard weed. A community of berry pickers is being transported back to Winesburg in full view of the lone man. A 'thin and girlish' voice from those berry pickers 'commands' the fat little old man to brush his hair. The fat little old man, whom we now know is called Wing Biddlebaum, then brushes his hair with his hands, even though he is completely, totally bald.

This short exchange could feel somewhat forced, didactic even: the cruelness of the berry pickers, their bullying comments to a lonely old fool. But in amongst all of this there are subtle introductions of themes. A picker attempts to drag a maiden away with him. The sentence before, the pickers are described as 'laughing and shouting boisterously'. Is this something innocent, a youthful game, or is there something more sinister to it? What is it, really, that we have just seen? And Biddlebaum's reaction to the joke is strange. He knows he has no hair: so why does he believe the word of a jesting berry picker? And yet, despite this confusion, our sympathies have now been engaged.

Biddlebaum is pacing his veranda because he is waiting for his friend, George Willard, a young man, a reporter. Or at least this is what Anderson makes one assume to be the case. It's that word again: 'something':

> With George Willard, son of Tom Willard, the proprietor of the New Willard House, he had formed something like a friendship. (27)

The meaning of 'something like a friendship' is, here, utterly contingent on the readers' willingness to take things at face value, at what *appears* to be the case. In the context of the story thus far, it would be fair to assume that the not-quite fullness of this friendship is due to Biddlebaum's social awkwardness, his 'ghostly band of doubts', his social exclusion from the town. But this isn't quite what Anderson tells us. Actually, it is Biddlebaum who has considered himself not 'a part of the town' where he's lived for twenty years; not the other way around. Similarly, people from the town come to him, but not vice versa. Anderson is keeping up our sympathy for Biddlebaum, but in no way absolving him. We are being given the very real opportunity to see two distinct, equally valid interpretations of Biddlebaum's character.

The central themes of the story – what is reported and what is truth, what we know and what we believe – play out fluently in both implication and explication in this opening section. We know that something isn't right, but are ready for the interlocutor, George Willard, to get to the bottom of whatever misdeeds or mistreatments have occurred. But this does not happen. We hear of an earlier meeting between the two, and the way Biddlebaum talked to the boy, but Willard does not come that evening. Instead Anderson introduces a cleave to the story, a conversational diversion.

> The story of Wing Biddlebaum is a story of hands. (28)

It is an authorial clearing of the throat, but also it is a clever sentence. There is, it suggests, both Biddlebaum's story and a story *about* Biddlebaum. And just as we expect to move on, perhaps, to the story proper, Anderson steps in again, pulls us away to comment on what is to come.

> The story of Wing Biddlebaum's hands is worth a book in itself. Sympathetically set forth it would tap many strange, beautiful qualities in obscure men. (29)

These could be taken as the words of a gossip, larding the importance of the story; but equally they could suggest further questions. If this story is worth a book in itself, why is it not getting it? And in its sympathy, how would it tap 'many strange, beautiful qualities'? And perhaps most pertinently, does this mean the story we are reading is not going to be sympathetic? It is a peculiarly brilliant piece of obfuscation. The doubts pile on to doubts – is anything in this story really to be trusted? – and they are capped by the next line. 'It is a job for a poet'. So not a novelist, a poet. Even the manner of the story's formal constraints is in flux; debateable even by the person telling it.

Close attention to these sentences is necessary to understand how Anderson has worked his concerns into the very fabric of the story, while not drawing attention to their placement. He conjures a climate of genteel distrust, one that is both pitiable – in the sense that we feel sorry for Biddlebaum – and also understandable – he is, after all, the unknowable recluse with the huge never-still hands who has picked 140 quarts of strawberries in one day. We still know there is a revelation to come. And we know that Biddlebaum's hands will be at the centre of it. We know that the story is called 'Hands' and that his is a story of hands. And so Anderson grows the menace of the hands.

That second interruption – 'The story of Wing Biddlebaum's hands is worth a book in itself' – separates the hands from the person: it is no longer the story of Biddlebaum but of Biddlebaum's hands. They are given a life of their own, an independence from the man himself. The town is proud of the hands, they are the source of Biddlebaum's 'fame'. They are, however, a constant burden on their owner, things to be hidden and watched over.

The scene in which Biddlebaum lays his hands on Willard takes place in flashback. It is a concise, yet no less dazzling, dramatization of a life lived in self-imposed exile, suddenly sensing its last chance at freedom.

> 'You are destroying yourself,' he cried. 'You have the
> inclination to be alone and to dream and you are afraid
> of dreams. You want to be like others in town here. You
> hear them talk and you try to imitate them.' (30)

What Biddlebaum says – its plaintiveness, its seething passion for life – is a challenge, a reproach and an inward accusation. There can be no doubt who he is really addressing.

But it is the chilling 'For once he forgot the hands' that becomes the pivot of the action. Biddlebaum can see his hands taking over, working their way to Willard's shoulders: twenty years of restraint and careful retreat from the world, and yet the hands do not forget, they have, as Willard thinks, 'something to do with his fear of... everyone.'

The story of Biddlebaum's hands is a story with many others within it, testimonies the veracity of which is hard to fathom. Once, Biddlebaum was a teacher called Myers. A man who was 'meant by nature to be a teacher of youth'. His teaching career, however, is threatened by a boy's complaint of being touched by Myers. Other voices join the accusations. Anderson however never gives an inkling of whether the charges are true. There is a novel here, as Anderson has already stated, a sweeping novel of misunderstanding, of dark desires and redemption. But that would be to give definitive answers. All we have here is interpretation. Our own suspicions.

With the knowledge of the past, but not whether it is to be trusted, we return to the unvisited Biddlebaum. Alone, eating the crumbs from a frugal dinner with 'unbelievable rapidity'. It is an ending that refuses to round out an easy conclusion. Is his greediness a sign of his moral degeneracy, or is this his hands once again working independently of his control? It is a final ambivalence, one last piece of guile from Anderson. It is a story that, like Biddlebaum, lives in its own shadows, in its own uncertainties. It is perhaps Anderson's most significant and challenging work.

And there is a lot of other work. Anderson's *Collected Stories* runs to 928 pages, yet few readers, if any, would make claims for all of his fiction. Critics are quick to point out the variant quality of his stories and novels – the two editions I have of *Winesburg, Ohio* in fact, both feature introductions apologising for the erratic nature of Anderson's writing.

Partly this is due to the completeness of *Winesburg, Ohio* itself – if it were published now it would certainly be marketed as a novel, or at least a novel in stories. Its successes – 'Mother', 'Nobody Knows', 'The Strength of God', 'The Untold Lie' and 'Death' – bolsters the more unremarkable and underwhelming tales. *Winesburg, Ohio* has an architecture which solidifies its constituent parts. Later collections are not so fortunate.

Without the unifying force of George Willard and the town of Winesburg, Anderson's stories are left to fend for themselves: alone and without safety net. In amongst them there are several that are easily the equal of Anderson's acclaimed early work; some that rival 'Hands' as his most effective pieces. In fact the story I would press on anyone interested in Anderson appears in his final volume of stories, *A Death in the Woods and Other Stories*. If 'Hands' is a more sensational exploration of identity and alienation, 'The Return' is more refined, more everyday. It is also, despite its Prohibition-era setting, almost furiously contemporary in tone.

'The Return', like the stories in *Winesburg, Ohio*, uses a third-person narration, but this is written closer to the characters, more tightly focused on thought, emotion and repercussion. John Holden has come home to Caxton to see his old town, his old friends. He is successful and lives in New York, hasn't been home in eighteen years. Anderson gives us him all in the first three lines:

> Eighteen years. Well, he was driving a good car, an expensive roadster. He was well clad, a rather solid, fine-looking man, not too heavy. When he had left the Middle-Western town to go live in New York City he was twenty-two and now, on his way back, he was forty. (Anderson 2006: 28)

Gone is the oral tradition, the declarative sentences. Coming after the 'Eighteen years.' The conversational 'well,' does not suggest a voice, however, more of a weighing of a thought. And the thoughts of a man who would probably describe himself as 'not too heavy'. Through this we know the kind of person we're dealing with. A prig and a bore and someone rather too pleased with himself. Someone who has let his success turn his own head. The opposite to the way we were sympathetically introduced to Wing Biddlebaum.

Immediately, Anderson subverts this. The second paragraph shows Holden as a man of self-doubt, of self-knowledge too. He worries he is only returning home to gloat, to tell his old friends of his good fortune. He had once done the same by writing letters to his friends back home. In the town where he has stopped for lunch en route to home, he has an epiphany. The letters were arrogant, self-absorbed affairs without so much of a 'I hope you are well' to pay lip service to an interest in their lives.

It's this moment, early in the story, which shows Anderson at his most subtle and affecting. The letters home are those of youth and those of boasting indifference. They are also projections of a self that Holden had yet to become. He does not mention in those letters that his uncle, who has set him up with a good job, 'had not been excessively fond of him'. Neither does he mention that his aunt seems disappointed with his conventionality. What we are seeing here is not the usual haven't-we-all-changed-so-much! side of a homecoming, but the fear that nothing much has changed. That we are the same person, making the same kind of mistakes.

Interestingly, at this point, Anderson breaks with the convention of putting thought inside speech marks, injecting Holden's inner feelings directly into the main narrative.

'Odd thoughts, eh? Well, what was a fellow to do? You had but the one life to live. You had to think of yourself.' (Anderson 2006: 31)

From this vantage point we know the lie of which he speaks, and he knows it too. There are so many lives to lead, the one in Caxton, the one in New York, the one that is to come. It is yet more self-deception, more curating of personal experience. It's a theme – the wish for, or even belief in, difference, but the inability to attain it – which runs through stories such as 'The Teacher' and 'The Philosopher' and brings us back to the epigraph of George Bellows – a person striving for something, though they know not what.

Holden though has more motives than he allows himself to realise. The death of his wife is dropped casually into the story, also his child's time away at camp. This is a man cast adrift and where else to go but the home he abandoned, the home that will welcome him as a hero, where a ball team will be playing and his childhood sweetheart will be unmarried. This is a home that never existed; a place that can never live up to this fevered and beautifully wrought fantasy.

'The Return' is consistently arresting because it refuses to follow any notion of the expected. Holden has second thoughts about heading to Caxton but arrives there nonetheless. The town is much the same as before, a few cosmetic changes but little else. The pined-for friends are nowhere to be seen; only a once-younger boy, now in his thirties and a drunk, remembers him. And the night he imagined – of catching up with friends and rekindling a lost romance – is destroyed in drink and confusion.

As the night progresses, we expect to meet Lillian, the great lost love. But, we only get a report of her: divorced and with her looks long behind her. We are left to follow the course of the evening in all of its frivolity and underlying sadness. The obvious course of the story has been thwarted and in doing so we see more of Holden, less of his fantasy life. Because in his home town, away from both his dreams and the reality of widowerhood, Holden is given a different path – a different opportunity. What could have been stale, predictable, is energised by Anderson's unusual choices, and by alternative scenarios.

It's the craft – and by craft I mean guile, cunning – of Anderson that so often makes the difference to his stories. Few writers are now influenced by Anderson's style and sentences, but his story construction, his building of narrative and understanding of how to use the simple to convey the multifarious remains remarkable. 'Hands' and 'The Return' are just two examples of this great writer's art, his generosity of spirit and his recognition of the quiet humanity of ordinary lives. There are many others. They are all after something. They are always after something.

Ten Essential Stories

'Hands' (1919)★
'Nobody Knows' (1919)
'The Strength Of God' (1919)
'Mother' (1919)
'The Untold Lie' (1919)
'I Want To Know Why' (1919)
'The Egg' (1921)
'Out Of Nowhere Into Nothing' (1921)
'Death In The Woods' (1933)
'The Return' (1933)★

Ali Smith

on

James Joyce

The Start of the Start of James Joyce's Fiction: Some Thoughts on the Opening Paragraphs of the First Three Stories in *Dubliners*

Is it possible to come at Joyce's work now fresh, to read it free of all the critical baggage of epiphany and epicleti, the century's-worth of exegesis?

(In the piece below I'm honouring in spirit the chance encounter I had as a child of nine in the early 1970s with a book that happened to be in the cupboard above the bed in the bedroom I shared with my two much elder sisters. Fifteen years later when I was in my mid-twenties and a postgraduate student, sitting in a university library and reading the opening stories in *Dubliners* for what I believed was the first time, I realised that what I'd read as a small girl and what I had never forgotten, in fact still recalled vividly all that time after, because it had been so exotic to me in being such a true-seeming story, like no other story I'd ever read, particularly because it had seemed to my child self as recognisably strange and unexplained as life really was — was the second story in *Dubliners*, the one called 'An Encounter'.)

★

The three first stories of *Dubliners* are the only stories in the collection written in the first person (a mode Joyce only really uses elsewhere in his lyric poetry, or notably in Molly's monologue at the end of *Ulysses* – though it's also arguable that the whole of *Finnegans Wake* is written in a meld of first, second and third person dream-language). They're all, one way or another, concerned with the passage from innocence to knowledge, boyhood to adolescence. The first story concerns the death of a priest. The second story concerns a boy who takes a day off from from being educated by priests and gains an unexpected education. The third story concerns a boy growing up in the house of a dead priest, who learns the difference between real and ideal.

Each of them is an education in the ways not just narrative form but language itself works. Each of them addresses expectations about narrative, asks what a story is, what it could be, and – to some extent there is a moral inference in this – what it should be.

THE SISTERS

There was no hope for him this time: it was the third stroke. Night after night I had passed the house (it was vacation time) and studied the lighted square of window: and night after night I had found it lighted in the same way, faintly and evenly. If he was dead, I thought, I would see the reflection of candles on the darkened blind for I knew that two candles must be set at the head of a corpse. He had often said to me: I am *not long for this world*, and I had thought his words idle. Now I knew they were true. Every night as I gazed up at the window I said softly to myself the word *paralysis*. It had always sounded strangely in my ears, like the word *gnomon* in the Euclid and the word *simony* in the

Catechism. But now it sounded to me like the name of some maleficent and sinful being. It filled me with fear, and yet I longed to be nearer to it and to look upon its deadly work. (Joyce 2012: 1)

There was no hope: what a striking, damning opening phrase for a story, for a collection of stories, for a first book. This will turn out to be a book precisely about the loss of hope, about countless losses of hope across a city, a people and a time. In story after story it will be an inquiry into hopelessness and the dashing of hopes – but simultaneously an inquiry into what takes hope's place, what's there instead in the stripped-down pretentionless space of the loss.

It was the third stroke: this is of course a reference to the physical deterioration of the priest at the centre of this story. But at this stage it's just the second clause in a mysterious first sentence, and this more open context also suggests three strokes of the clock. In a book called 'Dubliners' at this point in time, the first sentence inevitably has a religious reference to the moment at which Christ gives up the ghost on the cross on Good Friday. (The stories will proceed, the inference is, from this heart of spiritual darkness toward a promised rebirth; for sure this collection will end both lyrically and ironically with a story specifically called 'The Dead', and specifically about a timeless passion, the kind of love that outlives the human brevity and dissolution with which this first paragraph, and this first story, is about to concern itself.)

Vacation time ... studied: the speaker is a student, and even in vacation time there's a state of studying, for him at least, that doesn't let up or end.

Night after night ... night after night: there is a hint of suspension suggested in the repetition here; it's also a question of the particular suspension between life and death.

<u>For I knew that two candles</u>: The story (and this whole collection) will be watchful from the start for the signs of, the conventions of, the ways of telling life and death.

<u>I had thought his words idle. Now I knew they were true</u>: Joyce is much taken up in this first paragraph with notions of idleness, work, truth and language – with the seeming idleness and the true working of words.

First he admits the truth of cliché and gifts truth back to cliché, or tired words and phrases (and the latter is something he will go on to do, by extravagant and exciting transformatory means, throughout all his fiction). Then he draws his reader's attention, in this paragraph about the signs of life and death and the larger questions surrounding issues of spiritual death, very specifically to three words, which he displays, clearly associatively, in the same italics as the dying man's cliché, *I am not long for this world*.

These three words *paralysis… gnomon… simony* are held in the questioning space of the paragraph (the lit or dark window), themselves suspended between this life and death. Next to the cliché they act as astonishing enliveners. The strangeness of the turn of thought of the speaker, evidently a student of some kind, actually calls studious attention to the strangeness of these words which 'sounded strangely to my ears' – there is a question of allowing words their strangeness, a strangeness which will alter expectations or contexts. Here their strangeness unfixes, takes the notion of being *not long for this world* and somehow both sidelines and surpasses it. <u>Paralysis</u> is a word (and a concept) which will echo through this collection. If idleness and paralysis are meant to be associated here, and if idle words can in the end be revealed as true working words all along, then maybe paralysis can also turn out to be a kind of activeness. <u>Gnomon</u> is a word that means several things. It can be the shadow-casting part of a sundial; it means an indicator; something which aids discovery; and it comes from the Greek for 'that which reveals'. There

94

will be revelation, and it will be done by shadow-work and will perhaps tell us something about time, what time it is, where we are in time. This particular indicator or gnomon lies succinctly between paralysis and <u>simony</u>, the term for paying or accepting money for spiritual services, a kind of prostitution of spirituality. This story (and collection) will somehow concern the (probably blasphemous and unacceptable) point at which the material and the spiritual words meet and have a two-way exchange.

<u>Maleficent and sinful being… deadly work</u>: this will be a story (and a book) about the magnetisms of words, their strangeness, their workings, their lively work, plus the attractions of the dead and the deadly, and also the ways we read and process longing and attraction.

Other thoughts about this story: why is it called 'The Sisters', when we don't get to the sisters (as characters) till halfway through the story, a story ostensibly about the relationship between an old priest and a young boy?

'The Sisters' is about going beyond your own concerns. It does also seem to be a story about a crevasse between male and female worlds, as well as about the broken state between spiritual expectation and human actuality, the human tendency towards imperfection, brokenness, decrepitude. Partly it's interesting to note that the stories throughout *Dubliners* tend formally to use their second halves or final sections to veer off into new territory which alters their beginnings or surprises those beginnings into new contexts.

But the expectation of story is what this story flouts, and the experience of reading this story in full is one of being diverted, present and alert, from where we thought we were going and via a process of elipsis, via attention to unexpected uses of light and shadow, via the making strange of words and the re-seeing of cliché, being gifted newly (or differently) opened eyes and ears. The narrator's senses open to be alert to the everyday elision and elipsis in people's speech, the inadvertent puns, the repulsive details that form a real education, and to the eyes-open sense of the word wake (Joyce's fiction begins with a wake and ends with a Wake, the huge act of dual demise /rebirth of the novel that takes the form of *Finnegans Wake:* 'Hohohoho, Mister Finn, you're going to be Mister Finnagain!')

'Such a beautiful corpse,' one of the sisters in 'The Sisters' says. The boy telling the story, a one-time student of the dead man, who told him 'stories about the catacombs and about Napoleon Bonaparte [...] the meaning of the different ceremonies of the Mass [...] the different vestments worn by the priest', stories of bones, rituals, vestments, conquerors and conquered, ends this story reporting to us the real strangeness of things – what he can hear, what he can see.

AN ENCOUNTER

It was Joe Dillon who introduced the *Wild West* to us. He had a little library made up of old numbers of *The Union Jack, Pluck,* and *The Halfpenny Marvel.* Every evening after school we met in his back garden and arranged Indian battles. He and his fat young brother Leo the idler held the loft of the stable while we tried to carry it by storm; or we fought a pitched battle on the grass. But, however well we fought, we never won siege or battle and all our bouts ended with Joe Dillon's war dance of victory. His parents went to eight-o'clock mass every morning in Gardiner Street and the peaceful odour of Mrs Dillon was prevalent in the hall of the house. But he played too fiercely for us who were younger and more timid. He looked like some kind of an Indian when he capered round the garden, an old tea-cosy on his head, beating a tin with his fist and yelling:

—Ya! yaka, yaka, yaka! (Joyce 2012: 10)

The opening of 'An Encounter' connects the reading experience to the fighting experience. Both here are matters of territory, adventure, courage and timidity, negotiation between wildness and civility, rules and 'unruliness.' Something about the fact that the reading experience takes its reader elsewhere makes this experience a matter of propriety and home, and also a battle which looks to be unwinnable.

It suggests a male world again separated from a more peaceful female (or at least more peaceful-smelling) world. At the head of this tale of battle, which opens on a childsplay too fierce for all but one of the children playing it (the one who'll go on, the story tells us straight after the above opening paragraph, unlikely though it seems, to become a priest), is a reading matter called *Union Jack* – the first of the volumes in a 'library […] of old numbers'. The territory line is marked from the start by this matter of nationality; this story will be full of similar, more or less casually-noted markers of division, between social classes, between countries, between familiar and foreign, Catholic and Protestant, those who 'know' and those who only pretend to, those who stay at home and those who venture abroad, people who're the right and who're the wrong sort.

So from the start this story's subject is reading matter and how it relates to reality, mystery, identity, the given shape of adventure – and a dividing line. What happens in the story is: some boys take time off school to find an 'adventure' but find instead an unexpected and anticlimactic experience. They happen to meet a stranger. The strangeness of this stranger brings about a subtle but huge change in understanding in one of the boys, the narrator, who has been longing for not just fictional adventure but 'real adventures to happen to myself.'

First the truants head for the docks, the quay, the edge of the city, where they have a look at 'the spectacle of Dublin's commerce' and plan to visit a place called the Pigeon House on an island; the narrator's companion, Mahoney, plans to take catapult pot-shots at some birds. But nothing more adventurous happens than a chasing of some ragged children and a cat, and the boys, in some disappointment, abandon their original plan to go farther.

It's in this disappointment that they encounter the strange man, whose eyes are the romanticised 'green' the narrator had imagined would be the colour of the eyes of sailors on the quay. This man, dressed in greenish black, first noticed by the narrator when he's chewing 'one of those green stems' of grass 'on which girls tell fortunes' (i.e. in a repeated emphasis on a colour suggesting both Ireland itself and a combination of naivety, rottenness, fecundity, futurity) talks first about boyhood and books in a conventional way that leaves the boys 'bored' and our narrator full of divisiveness and pretension ('I pretended that I had read every book he mentioned […] I was afraid the man would think I was as stupid as Mahony').

The man then changes his subject, talks about 'sweethearts' in a sensual way that sends him off away from the boys but still in sight, to do something mysterious which our narrator refuses to look at or to enlighten us about. Is he masturbating? What he's doing is never made clear, only that our narrator will not look to see what he's doing. When the strange man returns and sits by the narrator and begins his monologue again, it has become a repetition of the words *boy, boys, girl, girls, whip, whipping, whipped*, and finally, *mystery*.

The word mystery is a loaded word for any Roman Catholic, another word for things sacramental. (See practically every other person who's ever written about Joyce for more on this.) But Joyce's shift here, in the encounter of 'An Encounter', from the cheap Wild West novels, turn of the century escapist magazines and detective mysteries which gave the boys their secretive relief from schoolwork, to the 'elaborate mystery' which the narrator senses 'unfolding', the unexpected 'adventure' of an encounter with a man who, in the aftermath of his own excitement and shame can't not connect sexuality and punishment, leaves the boy narrator ashamed at himself – at his own subterfuges and lies.

As he makes his escape from the man and his whip-mystery monologue, Joyce reveals the narrator in the process of understanding his own tendency to despise, and despising instead his own judgementalism, the division-making in himself. The story's end is masterfully subtle, a different kind of climax and certainly an unexpected narrative climax.

'An Encounter' is above all a story *about* the reading encounter, about what might constitute a 'real' reading experience or adventure, especially when it comes to escapism, freedom, truth. Its 'mystery' is allied to the man's seedy act, whatever it is. Countless critics have written about the difficulties Joyce had in publishing *Dubliners* as a collection. These stemmed, among other things, from his refusal (regardless of publishers' fears of being sued for obscenity) to tone down or edit or alter what happens, and what the narrator refuses to look at, in 'An Encounter'. It was, you might say, quite a battle; this collection, written in the main between 1904 and 1906, didn't see publication till a decade after its first stories were written.

At the centre of this story of what's permitted and what's repressed, what divides and what unites, the narrator on his way to this 'real adventure' stops and sits on a bridge, the bridge (as it were) between school and the rest of the world, between conventional restraint and what seems like wide-open possibility.

Before the disappointment, the anticlimactic climax of what really happens, Joyce gifts his green schoolboy narrator a moment of pure happiness unlike anything else in *Dubliners*. 'All the branches of the tall trees which lined the mall were gay with little light green leaves and the sunlight slanted through them on to the water. The granite stone of the bridge was beginning to be warm and I began to pat it with my hands in time to an air in my head. I was very happy.'

Then Joyce sets the cat among the pigeons; drops the real in among the cheap secrets, dead histories, cheap mysteries; plants the seedy, unsayably mysterious in among the clichés. In the brief space of this single short story a much larger freedom's been dared and the reading encounter itself has greened and bloomed into something truly wild and truly (until this story) unimaginable: an act of pioneering, a writing of a whole new shocked and wakened place of knowing, understanding, discovery and possibility.

ARABY

> North Richmond Street, being blind, was a quiet street except at the hour when the Christian Brothers' School set the boys free. An uninhabited house of two storeys stood at the blind end, detached from its neighbours in a square ground. The other houses of the street, conscious of decent lives within them, gazed at one another with brown imperturbable faces. (Joyce 2012: 19)

Does a place have eyes? What constitutes the vision of a place?

The first paragraph of Araby, the third story in the collection, and the last in the opening trilogy of first person meditations on coming of age, shifts in its three sentences from literal to metaphorical in a way that the stories before have completely avoided.

It juggles this possibility in its first five words, 'North Richmond Street, being blind'. It allows the use of 'blind' to settle into something closer to literal, cul-de-sac or dead end. The next sentence is literal. The third colours the first two sentences with its anthropomorphism, as if houses and places have consciousness and senses after all (as hinted in the first five words). Houses, in the third, even have faces, and all of this is something to do with decency and imperturbability.

So this will be a story about blindness and seeing, but it will also be a story about literary mode. Will it be about how we inhabit our houses, and also how the places we inhabit come alive via our inhabiting them? There's also a moment in the first sentence where sight and sound are linked, in the freeing of the senses when the boys are released not just from school but from malehood, and from Christianity. Will this be a story about being set free, and about the sight and hearing such liberation restores?

This is a story about books and learning, like the first two stories – but it will come after the other two with its eyes open as to figuration and metaphor. The boy narrator in Araby is growing up in the house of a dead priest. The literal books in this story (the dead priest has been survived by an old rusty bike pump which the boy finds in the garden, and some old damp books) are a romance, a devotional, and a memoir thriller from 50 years ago.

The description of the neighbourhood is, in comparison to the stories which came before, rich and leisured, memoir-like and a little damp itself; this narrator is drawn to fin-de-siècle colours (yellow book, violet sky); but there's the same slight catch in this prose of possible ambiguity, possible parody as is there in the story's first five words. 'The career of our play brought us through the dark muddy lanes behind the houses where we ran the gantlet of the rough tribes from the cottages, to the back doors of the dark dripping gardens where odours arose from the ashpits, to the dark odorous stables where a coachman smoothed and combed the horse or shook music from the buckled harness.' The passage is a conscious gorgeous prose of gauntlets and horses regardless of its ashpits, pleased with its own assonances ('odours arose', 'shook music', the drip of repetition, 'dark […] odours' cupped into 'dark odorous').

'Araby', with its title which can sound on the one hand like eastern exotica and on the other like some kind of makeshift adjective (arab-y), concerns a boy in the first throes of love, whose world is coloured by the light coming off a girl. When this girl eventually exchanges a word with him, it's to say she wishes she could go to Araby, but she can't, she's not free. He tells her if he goes he'll bring her something back. Where 'An Encounter' sent its narrator in search of the Wild West, this story sends its protagonist in search of the imagined East, but in reality to a Saturday night bazaar in the city.

He hides behind a blind and watches her in the house opposite. She's blind to him doing this, and in any case she's all images of fastening and imprisonment (the rope of her hair) and fastenings (the bracelet on her arm), always seen behind railings and pulled-down blinds. But her image makes the boy separate, apart, distanced in the general noise of the city. 'Her name was like a summons to all my foolish blood.' In fact the image of the girl turns him into an instrument:

> Her image accompanied me even in places the most hostile to romance [...] when my aunt went marketing [...] we walked through the flaring streets jostled by drunken men and bargaining women, amid the curses of labourers, the shrill litanies of shop-boys [...] the nasal chanting of street-singers who sang a come-all-you about O'Donovan Rossa, or a ballad about the troubles in our native land. These noises converged in a single sensation of life for me [...] Her name sprang to my lips at moments in strange prayers and praises which I myself did not understand [...] But my body was like a harp and her words and gestures were like fingers running upon the wires. (Joyce 2012: 20-21)

The instrument he becomes in this musical street is the symbol of Ireland itself – but a symbol which can't understand itself, can't hear the difference between curse and prayer and one which perceives the troubles as no more than a ballad.

But 'Araby''s purpose, from the start, has been about

drawing attention to blind and seeing states. 'I was thankful that I could see so little,' the boy says at one point, in a paragraph which begins as if it's going somewhere narrative but proceeds, like a Joycean joke, to go nowhere, to record nothing but the boy's self-indulgent vagary. Like this, everything in this story is a puncturing – one that understands the draw of, the richness of indulgence, but is keen to draw attention to the non-eventness of all things Araby. It's a story as gorgeous in its flat realisms as it is in its assonances, the fin-de-siècle yellowing of its own language. The evening he spends waiting so he can go to the bazaar is beset with irrelevant realisms and he gets to Araby so late that it's already nearly closed; then it costs him a lot to go in, and he buys nothing. A great deal of the detail of the final two pages is taken up with the literal cost of things. The foreignness of the bazaar is, the boy finds, no more foreign to Ireland than Englishness – a complicated enough realisation when it comes to the places romance and colonialisation meet. Finally the lights of Araby are switched off and the story ends. 'I heard a voice call from one end of the gallery that the light was out. The upper part of the hall was now completely dark.' The light Joyce throws on the boy's (and any culture's) tendency towards romanticism is a revelation of such darkness. It's this darkness that enables the boy to see and to reflect. 'Gazing up into the darkness I saw myself.' (p. 25)

His eyes, in this dark mirror, Joyce writes, 'burned with anguish and anger.' 'Araby' is a burning little darkness of a story, an incendiary rejection of outmoded language, a disaffecting exercise in shedding the vanity of expectations brought to both story and life, and one which insists, with all the fury of a narrator faced with his own humiliation, that any burning we do is with an energy which means the opposite of blindness, one that shows us how to see and how to hear who and where we are, even in the dark.

From this point onwards any *bildungsroman* about it is over. The stories in the collection make their subject other Dubliners.

Fifteen Essential Stories

'The Sisters' (1914)★
'An Encounter' (1914)★
'Araby' (1914)★
'Eveline' (1914)
'After the Race' (1914)
'Two Gallants' (1914)
'The Boarding House' (1914)
'A Little Cloud' (1914)
'Counterparts' (1914)
'Clay' (1914)
'A Painful Case' (1914)
'Ivy Day in the Committe Room' (1914)
'A Mother' (1914)
'Grace' (1914)
'The Dead' (1914)

Toby Litt

on

Franz Kafka

I HAVE AVOIDED writing about Kafka. A few years ago, Lawrence Norfolk invited me to contribute to a website. Writers were offering reactions to Kafka's long aphorism or short story about never getting to the next village. I'm afraid I ignored Lawrence Norfolk's invitation. Footnotes to Shakespeare are fine and very often dandy. We riff off *The Tempest* endlessly. And because no-one expects something significant to occur, there is no humiliation in adding nothing. A footnote to *The Tempest* may be worth writing, and will join an established society of footnotes. All that has barnacled onto Kafka could be scraped away, without loss. This isn't to say I am not grateful for what Walter Benjamin wrote. Or that Auden didn't have insight. Or that I learned nothing from Deleuze and Guattari. But Kafka is not sociable, like Shakespeare. His illuminators are a crowd of solipsists. And so I have avoided writing about Kafka. Because – put as simply as I can – Kakfa writes to make writing about Kafka impossible. This is absolutely not his main aim; that, I think, stays within the reader and their possibility-of-a-soul. Kafka's main thrust is toward inscrutability. He wants to open out possibilities so infinite that the original wanting is entirely moot, and the opening eternally backgrounded. He makes statements the end of which we can never hope to reach. For example, 'Before the Law'. I would quote 'Before the Law' in its entirety. Quote it twice. Instead, I will assume you have dutifully reread it in-between the previous sentence and this one. Or, at least, you have recalled some of the abysmal horror of it. Kafka makes statements the end of which we can never reach. In this, he is comparable to Emily Dickinson and who else? William Blake in 'The Proverbs of Hell'? Zeno? Heraclitus? Sappho? A few other absolutists. Yet Kafka is social. He came from alleys not the sun. And I am sure a third-hand acquaintance with the Jewish theatres of Praha, in Kafka's enthusiastic time, would not be meaningless. And a close textual reading through nothing but Torah might be more pointlessly correct than any other. And Robert Walser, Bruno Schulz, Isaac Babel, are in worthwhile correspondence. But my experience of reading Kafka is that he places me far. Not *far from*. He places me within a far relating only to itself.

This is not quite the far of the story within a story within a story we reach in 'Description of a Struggle' – the universe within a universe within a universe. At this early stage (1904–5), Kafka's far still has some tenuous connection to our near. But unities of time and space have become moot, ridiculous. If you wanted to be straightforward, you could say 'Description of a Struggle' is a great fantasy story, a piggyback *Alice's Adventures in Wonderland*. At points it reads, very strangely, as a parody of Chekhov. The tragic timidity of Chekhov's characters ('Live!' we beseech the page, like Henry James's Strether, 'Live all you can; it's a mistake not to.') becomes, through Kafka, the tragic timidity of Chekhov the creator. If only his young men had been able to levitate! If only they could have touched the lamp-posts beside the horizon! If only they had dream-visited otherworlds, not shabby Moscow! How much further into their predicaments they would have gone – and we would have gone with them! This is, on Kafka's part, creative misprison. It's a mutant

Chekhov he presents – distended, involuted, irresponsible, cute. But this is almost certainly completely wrong.

I do not know. This essay could come down to just that. I have avoided writing about Kafka because *I do not know – I do not know* where he is; *I do not know* what to say; *I do not know* what I do not know about Kafka. My suspicion is, *I do not know* because Kafka did not want me or any reader to know. At my most pissed off with him, I look at his stories and novels as clockwork contraptions for making mystification. This is the allegorical reading of 'In the Penal Colony' – and in this tale the mystification is figured as excrutiation. As a quick aside, I don't find Kafka a hoot. Some readers think this is the true test of whether you 'get it'. Does *The Trial* make you laugh out loud? With me, no. Is 'Metamorphosis' funny? For me, no. Kakfa makes me more profoundly anxious than any other writer. I am pretending to take a stroll, across a void, because the *far* is all around me in every direction – compass points, up and down. As another quick aside, I only read Kafka in English. How can I know if I could even tolerate Kafka's German prose? I know Willa and Edwin Muir. I know Tania and James Stern. I know Malcolm Pasley. (And I give them all my truest thanks.) At my most pissed off with my English-rendered Kafka, I think of Auden's definition of a poem as a 'verbal contraption'. The word contains both con and trap. At my most pissed off – and Kafka pisses me off more than any other writer – I view each sentence as both a con and a trap. Involutions of a certain sort imply the infinite. Here is false scripture, pimping off the Biblical and the Toraic. Here is pseudo-profundity, confusing Confucius and dumbing down the Dao. Here is profound shock, but only of a routine short circuit:

> 'The crows maintain that a single crow could destroy the heavens. There is no doubt of that, but it proves nothing against the heavens, for heaven simply means:

the impossibility of crows.' (Zürau Aphorism #32; Kafka 2002: 84)

He pulls the carpet, and the floor, and the earth out from under our feet; they are still there, draped, behind his back:

'Leopards break into the temple and drink the sacrificial vessels dry; this is repeated over and over again; finally it can be calculated in advance and it becomes a part of the ceremony.' (#20, Kafka 2002: 82)

But the aphorism I think about most often halts me in my annoyance. Restores me to loyalty and awe. Here is a sternness that doesn't seek publicity. Here, the con is internalized as conscience. Here, the trap is experienced from within. Kafka does, I sense, laugh at himself:

'There are two cardinal human sins from which all others derive: impatience and indolence. Because of impatience they were expelled from Paradise, because of indolence they do not return. But perhaps there is only one cardinal sin: impatience. Because of impatience, they were expelled, because of impatience, they do not return.' (#3, Kafka 2002: 79)

I have avoided writing about Kafka, but I have tried to write through him, off him. I have written stories I could not have written without the stories referred to in this essay: 'Investigations of a Dog', 'The Burrow', 'The Problem of Our Laws'. In my stories, I was trying to write Literature. (What a shaming confession.)

Kafka's contraptions seem, when I have ceased to be pissed off, worthwhile. They are Literature in a very high form.

Two examples will do: 'Investigations of a Dog' and 'The Burrow'. Here, unlike most writers, Kafka does not seem to be writing toward something. In both stories, the opening sentence is a foreclosure. 'How much my life has changed, and yet how unchanged it has remained at bottom!' and 'I have completed the construction of my burrow, and it seems to be successful.' These remind me of Jane Austen's perversely absolute negation, at the beginning of *Persuasion*, of one character's possibility of any development or change: 'Vanity was the beginning and the end of Sir Walter Elliot's character...' Where to go from there? Nothing so crass as an arc or a journey or a redemption. And Kafka's investigating dog and burrowing creature get nothing of that sort. By this point in his writing (1922-24), Kafka is only interested, on the page, in exploring *states* – almost, in exploring *stasis*. What happens within the reader, though, the vast shifts and splinterings and abandonments of hope, is something entirely different. These stories are often referred to as failures – worse, as boring or incompetent failures. They have nothing like the economy and elegance of 'In the Penal Colony' or 'Metamorphosis'. Traditional values like this have been departed from. We are in the middle of a far with no edge. These stories read, critics say, as first drafts. Their effects are insufficiently calculated. They go on for too long. But, for my Kafka, calculable effects are negligible as compared to incalculable ones. 'In the Penal Colony' and 'Metamorphosis' are agonies we witness; 'Investigations of a Dog' and 'The Burrow' engulf us in our own passions.

Today, I was trying to write a definition of that old-fashioned value, Literature with a capital L.

Literature is not Literary Fiction. That is not my definition, but it's a place to start because it's the place we have to start. The marketplace, etcetera.

Literary Fiction is read as the attempt to write Literature, and Literature is recapitulated as the Literary Fiction of the past.

I propose Three Ways to Tell Literature from Literary Fiction.

1. Literature requires rereading.
2. Literature reinvents reading.
3. Literature reconfigures the reader.

At a later point, I am going to reconfigure the word 'reconfigures'; for now, I am going to unpick each proposition.

Literature requires rereading

A book that requires rereading is, in some ways, radically unsatisfying. It will not please the market. It will not please the majority of readers.

Most Genre Fiction is written expressly for a single reading; most Literary Fiction is written implicitly not to be read at all.

If Literary Fiction is not read, then it can – without difficulty – be pointed to as Contemporary Literature. And then, because we can point to Contemporary Literature and next year more Contemporary Literature again, we need have no anxiety about the idea that we are not producing any Literature for those who follow us.

'Literature is writing that has the capacity to fascinate the future.' That was my old definition of Literature with a capital L.

Because you cannot hope to know what will fascinate the future, you cannot hope self-consciously to set out to write Literature.

To attempt to write Literature is to accept one's own bewilderment as one's start point.

Literary Fiction is Pin the Tail on the Donkey without being spun round and around, and without the blindfold.

Literature reinvents reading

One of the reasons you need to return to a book that is Literature is because, on the first reading, most of what it is doing is teaching you how to read it.

Your bewilderment on first reading Literature is one proof it is Literature.

There are lots of different ways of being bewildered; each writer of Literature will bewilder you uniquely.

First readers help later generations to be less bewildered. 'Kafka is this kind of writer,' they say. 'Kafka was a modernist.' 'Kakfa was a proto-absurdist.' 'Kafka was an existentialist.' 'Kafka was a very funny guy.' But, despite this, Kafka will never be anything less than a total mindfuck.

Literature reconfigures the reader

By temporarily or hopefully permanently changing how you read, Literature subtly changes how you are.

How you read affects how you read the world; but this is far too utilitarian. Kafka is not self-help. Kafka is anti-self-help.

You are an established fact. Literature makes you realise that you are not an established fact.

Perhaps I should not have said, 'Literature reconfigures the reader.'

Perhaps I should have said, 'Literature rediscovers the reader.'

No, perhaps I should have said, 'Literature resurrects the reader.'

Of course, Literature, in attempting-to-be-post-Judeo-Christian, needs to rival the promises of the Old Testament and the fulfilments (or not) of Christ.

Without being heretical, Literature loses a major part of its reason for being.

(Kakfa wants to relate to St Paul; Kafka desires heresy.)

Some definitions of Literature with a capital L

Literature is a refusal to accept a generalized view of what is.

(Too unspecific, this. Philosophy might be covered. Or contrarianism.)

Literature is the written record of unprecedented souls.

(Too elevated.)

Literature is a form of perfectly accomplished bewilderment.

Or, Literature is a perfectly accomplished form of bewilderment.

This is why – The pleasures of Literary Fiction are the pleasures of orientation; the pleasures of Literature are the pleasures of bewilderment.

What do you say, while you are being bewildered? What do you say afterwards? *I do not know. I do not know.*

The stories I have chosen to mention below are the ones that make me say *I do not know* most powerfully. Because, with several of them, *I do not know* if they are good or bad, or whether that even matters. *I suspect* they are unreasonably great.

I would like to say something about what *I suspect* can be learned from Kafka. And, as a preface to this, you need to read Kafka's description of his ideal, from a letter to Felice Bauer, January 14th, 1913:

'I have often thought that the best mode of life for me would be to sit in the innermost room of a locked cellar with my writing things and a lamp. Food would be brought and always put far away from my room, outside the cellar's outermost door. The walk to my food, in my dressing gown, through the vaulted cellars, would be my only exercise. I would then return to my table, eat slowly and with deliberation, and then start writing again at once. And how I would write! From what depths I would drag it up!'

This is a young man trying to impress a young woman. It is also a writer wishing to be simultaneously unconvincingly imprisoned ('outside the cellar's *outermost* door') and to be kept as a pet (Kafka's food materializes as mysteriously as that of the dogs' in 'Investigations of a Dog').

The writings of Kafka from which (*I suspect*) we have most to learn are his rhapsodies of perpetual clarification: 'Investigations of a Dog', 'The Problem of Our Laws', 'A Report to an Academy', 'A Hunger Artist', 'The Burrow'. In them, we do not behold the sentences of Flaubert – aspiring to be carved in marble, academized. Instead, we witness the as-live struggles of a meaningful animal – exhausted, hungry, short of breath – to express something of both imminent and immanent value.

The greatest writers, like the greatest athletes, are capable of great precision at great speed. It is their velocity of thought makes this possible. A writer can think far faster than Charlie Parker could play – yet Charlie Parker is the best depiction I know of speed-of-thought. With great writing we travel further, in each sentence, than seems possible. Words are doing more than words can do – without some kind of influx of the miraculous; not *miracle*, because that suggests tableaux and adoration. This is pure flow, which we – lucky – follow. The model is 'To be or not to be...'

Reading this kind of writing, our breathing comes more in sync with the writer's. The breath in a Flaubert sentence is many-times breathed; in Kafka, there seems to be an unnatural amount of chill oxygen – because we are in the giddy, gainful, terrifying phase of hyperventilation. The throat is scoured. All Kafka's stories read as if written by a guest of the Ice Queen. The air stabs us with lung-clarity. The heart vomits thick blood.

I think Kafka goes headlong into his writing. He bends forwards and his head fully enters the paper of the page and he lifts up into a perfect handstand on the desk. Then his legs start to sprint through the empty air as he feels himself beginning to drown.

Everything he wrote was a transcription of this experience. He was not a palimpsest-maker. He attempted to do an absolute draft, not a first or a second. He performed himself, or his persona, directly into the page. His technique (as such) was developed to keep up with this. Not a follower of a dutiful routine; shamefully more like an inspired poet. Which leaves the wannabe writer little of use from which to learn. This method is irresponsible. 'When it arrives, go with it.' And this method is more likely than any other to produce stream-of-pompousness shit; sub-Beat extemporizing on the tedious self; whatever's echoing in your unvoid head. This method depends on preparation. The real work must go into revising the possibility-of-a-soul. Unfortunately, you'd have to call this spiritual discipline.

Kafka finds his world populated by intolerable things. It is through the absoluteness of his avoidances that we most know him. He sprints and dodges, dead-ends and doubles back − ridiculous upside-down legs, kicking the shit out of the icy air. What would be a default for us is anathema for him. And, in conclusion, he does not write what other writers write.

Kafka created subject areas where other writers saw only frustration. He, so far as I know, lived through the Great War without allowing it to nudge his hierarchy of what is fictionally important. If inscrutability was his thrust, he went further out into it than anyone but Shakespeare. How did he achieve this eminence? You already know that *I do not know.*

However, *I suspect* it was partly because he believed *everything* depended on what he wrote; and not a reasonable *everything.*

Ten Essential Stories

'The Wish to Be a Red Indian' (1912)
'Description of a Struggle' (1912)★
'Metamorphosis' (1915)
'Before the Law' (1915)
'In the Penal Colony' (1919)
'The Bucket Rider' (1921)
'The Problem of Our Laws' (1920, published 1931)
'A Hunger Artist' (1922)
'Investigations of a Dog' (1922, published 1931)
'The Burrow' (1924, published 1931)

David Constantine

on

D.H. Lawrence

The Making of Consciousness

In Doris Lessing's *The Golden Notebook* Anna Wulf notes 'Literature is analysis after the event.' This – Anna feels – is a matter for regret (Lessing, 210 and 217). Robert Lowell said: 'A poem is an event, not the record of an event' (Lowell, 304). Anna, and her author, want a literature, a kind of fiction, which will be, as Lowell says the poem is, the event itself. Lawrence wrote (in 'Morality and the Novel'): 'The business of art is to reveal the relation between man and his circumambient universe, at the living moment.' And in fiction, poetry, essays and letters, that is what he did.

Such writing is the process itself by which the relationship between man and the universe is revealed: the relations among humans, but also (think of the poems in *Birds, Beasts and Flowers*) the relations – vitally effective mutual relations – of humans with fellow living things in all manner of landscapes. And in practice Lawrence does more than *reveal* the relationship, if by that is meant show what is already there. By the act of writing he is a participant in the very making of it. His writing is a means by which our relations with one another and with the world around us may be understood, but also, if necessary (and it will very often, pehaps even always, be necessary) the means by which they may be

117

opened up to change. He says of van Gogh: 'When van Gogh paints sunflowers, he reveals, or achieves, the vivid relation between himself, as man, and the sunflower, as sunflower, at that quick moment of time' (*Criticism*, 108). Lawrence writes like that: achieving relationship, showing it, momentarily. Lawrence was a great admirer of Walt Whitman – 'he is so near the quick', (*Criticism*, 84-89) – and in his essay 'Poetry of the Present' (written as the War ended, when, as he believed, a new consciousness had to be brought into being or humanity would not survive) he announced the poetics which in his writing he was already practising: that of touching on the moment, showing flux, change, the life that, for it to be life, can never settle. Naturally such writing cannot even desire to arrive at a fixed point. It arrives at something tentative, provisional, opening. There is no closure in Lawrence's writing because there is none in life. Anna Wulf again: 'It ocurred to me […] that the raw unfinished quality in my life was precisely what was valuable in it.'

'ART FOR MY SAKE'

Against 'Art for Art's Sake', Lawrence set his own motto: 'Art for my sake' (Letter to Ernest Collings, 24 Dec. 1912). To an extraordinary degree he was a writer who by writing tried to understand and fashion his self-identity. Writing, for him, was a matter of life or death. After bad pneumonia in 1911, after its crisis, he sat up in bed writing 'The Shades of Spring', which is one of two or three short stories 'on the way to' *Paul Morel*, which is itself on the way to *Sons and Lovers*. Aldous Huxley said of him: 'For Lawrence, existence was one continuous convalescence; it was as though he were newly re-born from a mortal illness every day of his life' (*Letters*, 1265). And in 1926, in the essay 'Getting on', he said himself, 'If I had never written, I probably should have died soon. The being able to express one's soul keeps one alive' (Worthen, 326). The continual revisions and rewritings – the three distinct versions of *Lady Chatterly's Lover*, for example – are compulsive efforts to say the thing better, to get nearer the truth of it, to be enabled to live in that truth.

THE REFUSAL OF CONSCIOUSNESS

In 'The Prussian Officer' the officer in question thoroughly violates the liberty, dignity, and individual identity of his servant – slaps him, makes fun of him, thwarts and insults him, and, utterly letting go, when he turns away with his arms full of dishes, kicks him, so that he stumbles and drops them, then kicks him again and again. And as soon as the young man has gone, this officer who has command over him, summons up all his resources of self-discipline to suppress the consciousness of what he has just done:

> The officer, left alone, held himself rigid, to prevent himself from thinking. His instinct warned him that he must not think. Deep inside him was the intense gratification of his passion, still working powerfully. Then there was a counter-action, a horrible breaking down of something inside him, a whole agony of reaction. He stood there for an hour motionless, a chaos of sensations, but rigid with a will to keep blank his consciousness, to prevent his mind grasping. And he held himself so until the worst of the stress had passed, when he began to drink, drank himself to an intoxication, till he slept obliterated. When he woke in the morning he was shaken to the base of his nature. But he had fought off the realisation of what he had done. He had prevented his mind from taking it in, had suppressed it along with his instincts, and the conscious man had nothing to do with it. He felt only as after a bout of intoxication, weak, but the affair itself all dim and not to be recovered. Of the drunkenness of his passion he successfully refused remembrance. (Lawrence 1968: II, 103)

Lawrence was in Germany in 1912, on a pre-marriage honeymoon with Frieda Weekly (née von Richthofen). He wrote 'The Prussian Officer', and another story, 'The Thorn in the Flesh', which moves in the same ethos of military command, brutality and the bid for a life of one's own, in 1913. They are prescient stories.

THE NEED TO BECOME CONSCIOUS

As the First World War proceeded, Lawrence felt certain that the civilized world's old idea and understanding of itself could not hold. All his writing, the stuff of it and the very making of sentences, was thereafter a struggle to fashion a consciousness adequate to the fact of the War, so that people should think, feel and live differently after and in accordance with that fact. He wrote:

> It was so foul, and humanity in Europe fell suddenly into such ignominy and inhuman ghastliness, that we shall *never* fully realize what it was. We just cannot bear it. We haven't the soul-strength to contemplate it.
>
> And yet, humanity can only finally conquer by realizing. It is human destiny, since Man fell into consciousness and self-consciousness, that we can only go forward step by step through realization, full, bitter, conscious realization. (Introduction to 'Memoirs of the Foreign Legion', II, 357-8)

He said (in 'Morality and the Novel'): 'As mankind is always struggling in the toils of old relationships, art is always ahead of the 'times', which themselves are always far in the rear of the living moment.' In *Mrs Dalloway* Virginia Woolf showed a post-war society set on resuming its old course of life as though nothing had changed. But one character, Septimus, can't resume. In him the fact of the War is unliveable with. He kills himself.

D.H. LAWRENCE

First-Person or Third-Person Narration?

Of all Lawrence's novels only one, the first (*The White Peacock*) is written in the first person; none of his novellas is; and of his 60 or more short stories, only six are. I should say that first-person narration is less suited than third to the making of consciousness by the act of – and in the process of – writing. A first-person narrative – the story is finished, in the past, a participant-narrator is telling it – will easily become 'analysis after the event'. Lawrence's characteristic narrative voice is third-person omniscient; but it is an omniscience which he deliberately fragments, makes partial, just as the driving interest of the story dicates. That is to say, he moves around as he pleases, he may disregard the inner workings of some characters entirely, to concentrate on those or on the one he most wishes to bring into fuller consciousness. He may take up a character for close scrutiny, then drop him or her for someone else. This strategy – of a sovereign freedom – is itself a maker of the sense of the stories. Their restlessness, their quick shifting of perspectives, their sometimes headlong following through, their breaking off , to leave an outcome open: that way of narrating fits and reinforces the belief that the lives of humans living intensely, at crises, in the possibility or the necessity of change, are like that.

'Odour of Chrysanthemums': Bringing it Home

In his workroom Bertolt Brecht had always visible this dictum derived by Lenin out of Hegel:'Truth is concrete'. For the writer this means that the truth of the writing – drama, poetry, prose-fiction, essay – must be made concrete, must be realized, and so brought home to the reader, in substantial, graspable, physically telling form. And that is Lawrence's way. Most of his stories, and many individual chapters of his novels, bring a truth into life through an image, or an 'image-situation', a nexus out of which much of the story's total sense may be developed.

In 'Odour of Chrysanthemums' (1909-11) those flowers, recurring, are not symbols, they are not there as mere instruments, pointing to something else beyond themselves. They are moments, real concrete details around which the story's developing sense accrues, precipitates. At dusk the woman goes out into the wintry garden ('beside the path hung dishevelled pink chrysanthemums') to call in her son. Then:

> As they went slowly towards the house he tore at the ragged wisps of chrysanthemums and dropped the petals in handfuls along the path.
> 'Don't do that – it looks nasty,' said his mother. He refrained, and she, suddenly pitiful, broke off a twig with three or four wan flowers and held them against her face. When mother and son reached the yard her hand hesitated, and instead of laying the flower aside, she pushed it in her apron-band. (II, 284)

Much of the sense of that passage, a sense that will inform the rest of the story, is in those two words between commas: 'suddenly pitiful'. She pities the boy, who, dressed in clothes 'cut down from a man's' (II, 284), already suffers from the father's drinking and coming home late, and will suffer worse, as she will, after he is brought home dead. She is herself pitiable, she holds the flowers as though for comfort against her face; and seeming to pity them too ('dishevelled', 'wan'), preserves them close to her body and brings them into the house. That small scene with the mother, the chrysanthemums and the son, is soon followed by another, even more luminous, with the daughter replacing him. The woman reaches up to light the lamp. As she does so, 'her figure displayed itself just rounding with maternity'. She is pregnant – Lawrence *shows* it, does not *report* it – with a baby whose father is already dead. But what the girl sees is the flower – '"Oh, Mother [...] You've got a flower in your apron!" said the child, in a little rapture at this unusual event.' And to smell them, she puts her face against her mother's waist, who in the suspense of waiting for her husband, turning against him, irritably takes the flowers from her apron-band, whereupon the child seizes them, puts them to her lips, murmuring "'Don't they smell beautiful!'". Further sense is then revealed in them by the mother's reply:

> 'No,' she said, 'not to me. It was chrysanthemums when I married him, and chrysanthemums when you were born, and the first time they ever brought him home drunk, he'd got brown chrysanthemums in his button-hole.' (II, 288-9)

When they bring him home dead, there are two vases of pink chrysanthemums in the tiny parlour, 'a cold, deathly smell' of them (II, 296); one vase gets smashed in the manoeuvring with the stretcher and the flowers spill in their water on the floor.

In its entirety the story does what the flowers, occasion by occasion and as a series, do: it brings the truth closer and closer and, finally, home. The woman is waiting resentfully for her husband, the collier, to come home – drunk, as she expects. Much of the truth of their marriage is made palpable in that waiting; first in the exchanges with her father, then with her children. When the children have gone to bed, she goes out looking for him; then returns, to wait, now with her mother-in-law, and her anger shot through with anxiety. Then comes the thing itself, the dead man on a stretcher, intruded with difficulty down the step and into the cramped cold parlour. He is brought home, still warm, in his pit-dirt. Mother and wife, washing him, laying him out, are so close either side of him, their heads touch. That is a good image for what Lawrence's writing does: fetches things home, so that there is nothing between you and the bare facts, beautiful and terrible.

The wife, contemplating him in that terrible proximity, is forced into a further realization: of their essential apartness.

'In dread she turned her face away. The fact was too deadly. There had been nothing between them, and yet they had come together, exchanging their nakedness repeatedly' (II, 300). This sounds final, but it is well known that ideas of death, of the dead person, continue and change in the lives of the living. And there is much else in the story that denies the very idea of finality. The corpse is left in the parlour for the night. The children, compassionately told an untruth by their mother, next day will have to face the fact of death. In a few months she will bear another child. That unfinishedness at the ending is matched by one at the beginning: the wife's widowed father tells her (who already without knowing it is a widow) that he intends to re-marry.

DAUGHTERS OF THE VICAR

'Daughters of the Vicar' (1911, first called 'Two Marriages') is written in fifteen sections, in each one of which the story is advanced or, from various perspectives, reflected upon as briefly or extendedly as necessary. It is an effective form. Something is at work and at stake in every section, and their being numbered inclines us to give them all in turn their due attention. In the first, for example, less than three pages, the whole matrix of the story, that out of which it grows, is presented: 'The Reverend Ernest Lindley, aged twenty-seven, and newly married, came from his curacy in Suffolk to take charge of his church. He was just an ordinary young man, who had been to Cambridge and taken orders. His wife was a self-assured young woman, daughter of a Cambridge rector.' The church is new, built for a 'new, raw, disaffected population of colliers'. The Lindleys are poor. The vicar 'had no particular character, having always depended on his position in society to give him position among men. Now he was so poor, he had no social standing…' (I, 136-7). Consciously, without daring to acknowledge it, he soon hates the majority of his flock, and unconsciously he hates himself. His daughters are born into that bitter and oppressive nexus, and deal with it very differently.

Mrs Lindley bears several children – 'one every year; almost mechancially, she continued to perform her maternal duty, which was forced upon her' (I, 137) – but Lawrence is only interested in the two eldest, Mary and Louisa. He moves rapidly. In the second section Mary is 'about twenty years old'; in the next she is twenty-three, the father falls ill, he must have a curate to do his work. This curate is another Oxbridge man, 'not more than twenty-seven'. 'What a little abortion!' is Mrs Lindley's instant verdict on him (I, 145). But he will have an income of six or seven hundred a year for which, and in a willed self-violation, Mary marries him. And there Lawrence quits her for Louisa. Against her sister, shocked by that capitulation, Louisa asserts the premise of *her* life:

> They are wrong – they are all wrong. They have ground out their souls for what isn't worth anything, and there isn't a grain of love in them anywhere. And I *will* have love. They want us to deny it. They've never found it, so they want to say it doesn't exist. But I *will* have it. I *will* love – it is my birthright. I will love the man I marry – that is all I care about. (I, 155-6)

And her struggle to do just that, marry the miner Alfred Durant, get out of her class, break through his, defying her parents, forcing the issue in him, constitutes the rest, which is the bulk, of the story.

Louisa is there visiting when Alfred's father dies; also when his mother sickens – he comes home in his pit-dirt, she must wash his back since the dying mother can't; and there also when she dies. By chance, and also willing it, she is thrust into the proximity, the intimacy, the raw, appalling and beautiful truths of a life very far removed from that being lived by her sister and by her parents. And she loves the man whose hearth and home are there in this kind of truth. Still, like the vicar and the curate, he is himself class-bound, he cannot himself fetch Louisa into his life. He has fled once already, alone – to sea; he has a mind to flee again, alone – to Canada. Class is maintained by power, but also by acquiescence and *self*-subjugation. When his father dies, Alfred, still fearful, resists Louisa by retreating into his class, into self-subordination. Seeing that, she

> almost hated him. It was his way of getting out of it. She felt the cowardice of it, his calmly placing her in a superior class, and placing himself inaccessibly apart, in an inferior, as if she, the sentient woman who was fond of him, did not count. But she was not going to submit. Dogged in her heart she held on to him. (I, 150-1)

When his mother dies, Louisa's sister invites him to the vicarage, for some sympathy. 'Mr Lindley kept a special tone for him, kind, indulgent, but patronising' (I, 177). Alfred sits at their table, 'just submitting'. He leaves as soon as he can and thinks then only of getting right away, to Canada. Again, he allows class to threaten the attainment of what he needs for a proper life.

And it is Lousia who forces the change in him. She calls at his cottage two evenings later, he is alone and unwashed, their conversation fails. It is she who breaks through convention into the truth of their situation. '"Don't you want me?" she said helplessly.' Only then – she has put on her coat to leave, but has not fastened it – does he embrace her, smudging her face and blouse with the dirt from the mine. After that, it is only practicalities. They know what they want. They have to deal with her horrified family, they suffer its helpless revulsion, embarassment, hideous bad manners. But they know what they want, they will marry at once and leave for Canada.

Sentence by sentence, in fits and starts, with setbacks, hesitations, failures and revivals of courage, 'Daughters of the Vicar' enacts the struggle for a life you can call your own. As the story ends, the grounds having been put in place, the prospect of such a life is opening out.

D.H. LAWRENCE

The Horse Dealer's Daughter

Lawrence wrote 'The Horse Dealer's Daughter' in 1922. Soon after the mid-point of it comes this passage:

> He stood motionless as the small black figure walked slowly and deliberately towards the centre of the pond, very slowly, gradually moving deeper into the motionless water, and still moving forward as the water got up to her breast. Then he could see her no more in the dusk of the dead afternoon.
>
> 'There!' he exclaimed. 'Would you believe it?' (II, 449-50)

In essence the whole story is in those few lines: the stuff of it (the plot) and the very way of its being brought to life in sentences. The man, Jack Fergusson, stands watching the woman, Mabel Pervin, walk into the pond. That is a critical moment in the plot. But the long first sentence, in its advancing rhythm, its repetitions, by its very self, does a good deal more than tell us what is happening. Repeating the word 'motionless', for example, actually points up the difference between the motionlessness of a man watching a woman go in to drown herself and the motionlessness of the water in which she would do it. The strange quality of his motionlessness is articulated (after the simple and decisive second sentence) in the extreme strangeness of his exclamation. The only movement – she walks slowly and deliberately, she moves very slowly, gradually – is into the motionlessness of the water, and, unless *he* can move, into death. Reaching backwards and forwards, the whole story lives in that passage as palpably as does circulation through the body in a few felt pulses of the blood. And that is characteristic of Lawrence: the spirit of the particular story and the character of its writer are palpable throughout, in the shape and rhythms of every sentence. The story is a whole body, in character throughout.

In 'The Horse Dealer's Daughter', as in 'The Daughters of the Vicar', it is the woman who forces the issue; but before that crisis circumstances have assembled which make her realize that she must bid for a life worth living, *now*, or it will be too late. That urgency is clearer, we can more readily understand it, in Louisa's case: if she does not act, the man she loves, bound in a sort of cowardice, locked in his class, will depart, lessening her life and his own. Mabel Pervin, as *her* story opens, sits with her three brothers in the ruin of the household's fortune, and in a desultory and ineffectual fashion they make suggestions for her future. But Mabel takes no notice of them. 'They had talked at her and round her for so many years, that she hardly heard them at all' (II, 443). We know no better than her brothers do what Mabel needs; and sitting there with them at the end of a period of unsatisfactory life, perhaps she herself knows little, and that little only dumbly, of what at heart she needs. Dr Fergusson, who will rescue her from drowning, is introduced as the close friend of one of her brothers. The two men candidly admit their affection, and how they will suffer:

'Well, I shall miss yer, Freddy, boy,' said the young doctor.

'And I shall miss thee, Jack,' returned the other.

'Miss you like hell,' mused the doctor.

Fred Henry turned aside. There was nothing to say.

Then Mabel comes back into the room and with her Fergusson at once has an exchange in which there is no such confession but which, to him at least, is disturbing:

'What are *you* going to do, then, Miss Pervin?' asked Fergusson. 'Going to your sister's, are you?'

Mabel looked at him with her steady, dangerous eyes, that always made him uncomfortable, unsettling his superficial ease.

'No,' she said. (II, 445)

The ruin of the Pervin household, already accomplished, is only the premise of a more important breaking up – partings, unsettlings – out of which the real crisis of the story, that between Jack Fergusson and Mabel, will arise. First Lawrence tracks the man's movements towards it. Averted, impassive, Mabel goes about clearing the table, folding away the white cloth, putting on the chenille cloth in its place. But Fergusson watches her 'interestedly'. When she goes out, he turns to Fred Henry: 'What's she *going* to do then? And gets the answer 'Strike me if *I* know.' After which: 'There was a pause. Then the doctor stirred' (II, 446). In that small trance Fergusson shifts a little nearer to the outcome. Thus far the woman herself, perhaps even *to* herself, is a mystery.

That same afternoon, Mabel (another 27-year-old!) goes to tend the grave of her mother, who died when she was fourteen. Lawrence writes: 'She lived in the memory of her mother'; and indeed she is happier in the churchyard, tidying and adorning the grave, than anywhere else. 'There she always felt secure, as if no one could see her […] Under the shadow of the great looming church, among the graves, she felt immune from the world, reserved within the thick churchyard wall as in another country' (II, 447). In summary: 'The life she followed here in the world was far less real than the world of death she inherited from her mother' (II, 448). Dr Fergusson, setting off on his rounds from his house close to the church, sees her at work on her mother's grave.

> He slowed down as he walked, watched her as if spellbound.
> She lifted her eyes, feeling him looking. Their eyes met. And each looked again at once, each feeling, in some way, found out by the other. (II, 448)

Later, still visiting his patients as the afternoon ends, 'a slow, moist, heavy coldness sinking in and deadening all the faculties', he sees her walk into the pond 'in the green, shallow, soddened hollow of fields' below the house she and her brothers must now leave. He watches her, she seems not to know she is watched, so on the face of it her act is a step into death not into life. But she *is* seen, by him, and he hauls her out.

The crisis in 'The Horse Dealer's Daughter' comes as an imperative forcing. It is the reversal of *noli me tangere*, a summons to an ordeal: touch me. The act is not symbolic, if by that we should mean that it 'stands for' something else, some higher, deeper, more difficult-to-grasp experience. The circumstances in Lawrence's stories thicken into the figurative. They constitute the crisis and are the metaphor of it. They don't point away from themselves, they are the reality. But in those condensing circumstances the characters rise or sink or, let us just say, shift into their real lives' figurative dimension. They don't live less really for that. On the contrary, it is by virtue of their living really that they ever reach into that figurative dimension. The circumstances concentrate the life into revelation. They embody, indeed they force, a coming into consciousness. So Mabel Pervin, who has said nearly nothing, who has been talked at and around all her life, wakes out of her near-drowning and begins to realize things that matter. This whole passage of realization (II, 450-7) – seven pages, the long, close, culminating revelation and achievement of the characters' relationship – wants reading more attentively than I can here. It is the consequential carrying through of their earlier exchange of looks when each felt 'in some way, found out by the other'.

Waking, as in a fairy-tale, she asks him questions, seven in all, for her own enlightenment but also to drive him into enlightenment too. She asks, and is answered: Yes, he did go into the pond for her. Why did he? His answer and her response reveal a consciousness in her that is other, and deeper, than his:

'Because I didn't want you to do such a foolish thing,' he said.

'It wasn't foolish,' she said, still gazing at him as she lay on the floor, with a soft cushion under her head. 'It was the right thing to do. *I* knew best, then.'

Her final two questions push the process to its outcome. She realizes she is naked, wrapped in a blanket. She sees her clothes 'lying scattered'.

'Who undressed me?' she asked, her eyes resting full and inevitable on his face.
'I did,' he replied, 'to bring you round.'
For some moments she sat and gazed at him awfully, her lips parted.
'Do you love me, then?' she asked.

After that, forcing him further, she passes from questions to triumphant, confident, rhapsodic assertion, insisting, repeating against his reluctance to know it: 'You love me, you love me. I know you love me, I know.' She is ahead of Fergusson (she has been in deeper), she knows first. But then – Lawrence at his closest ('so near the quick') – the faith begins to leave her, she becomes hesitant, fearful, he sees and cannot bear the light of certainty 'dying from her face', and he breaks free of his own trammels and says, not to placate her but because it is the truth which she knew before he did: 'I love you! I love you!' in a voice 'unlike himself'. Not once does she say she loves him. It is manifest in her need to be assured that he loves her. So she forces him into the knowledge and the admission of the truth that will match her own truth, for the salvation of both their lives.

'JIMMY AND THE DESPERATE WOMAN'

Lawrence was in New Mexico when he wrote this story, in 1924. Like two or three others, it pillories John Middleton Murry, husband of Katherine Mansfield who had died the year before. Lawrence reaches out mercilessly across continents, back into the England he loved and loathed, and again into a setting (oppressive class) and a dynamic (the bid for breakthrough and freedom) that had become the chief motor of much of his writing.

The woman in question, Emilia Pinnegar, former-schoolteacher wife of a Yorkshire collier, may indeed be desperate; but so too, and essentially even more so, is Jimmy; and Lawrence applies the word to him as often as to her. Like the Reverend Lindley and his curate Massy, Jimmy is, 'terribly handicapped by his position'. By which is meant not just his being the editor of 'a high-class, rather high-brow, rather successful magazine' (III, 606), but also his class, his circle of friends, wherein he is very narowly circumscribed. And when he goes north and seeks out Mrs Pinnegar who has sent him some poems for his editorial consideration, Oxford adheres to him; his 'rather Oxfordy manner', his 'bit of an Oxford wriggle', his 'resonant Oxford voice' constitute his appearance and behaviour as a foreigner in the mining village. Wanting a room at the pub, when he does not at once get his own way, his voice becomes 'more expostulatingly Oxford than ever' (III, 615, 616, 622, 616).

Satire does tend to coarsen things, but in this case at least the fact that a man appears as a caricature is symptomatic of his failure to achieve an identity he can really call his own. He habitually deals (and is dealt with) in figures, emblems, labels for a life, not on the terms of life itself. He appears in the story as Pan, St Sebastian, the Oxford man, a Pilgrim Father, Mephistopheles. And having been left by his wife Clarissa, and pondering what sort of woman he might look for next, again he turns to figures. This unknown necessary replacement shall be a Tess, or a Gretchen, an unspoilt, unsophisticated woman of the people. And when Emilia Pinnegar pops up, though she is clearly not one of those, she does live in the north, and 'Jimmy had always had a mysterious feeling about these dark and rather dreadful mining villages in the north. He himself had scarcely set foot north of Oxford. He felt that these miners up there must be the real stuff' (III, 607). So she too belongs within an idea, in his head.

Altogether Jimmy's analysis of his problem, far from being a step on the way to its solution, is itself the problem. Which would not matter so much if it only damaged himself. But it also puts the woman at risk; and, very likely, as the story ends, it will seriously harm her. Closely tracking Jimmy's consciousness Lawrence makes clear just how desperate, and more importantly, how dangerous to other people, he is. His consciousness is only very partially open to the outside world. He only glances outside himself and then works up an idea which is, when set against the outside reality he has only squinted at, a dangerous fantasy. On the spur of the moment, having seen that Mrs Pinnegar is indeed unhappy in her situation, he suggests she come away to London and live with him. This is akin to the often sudden and drastic challenges issued by Lawrence's characters in their bids for freedom; but it is fatally different from, say, Louisa's to Alfred or Mabel Pervin's to Dr Jack Fergusson, in that it has no foundation in reality, in love, in just cause.

> Jimmy made this speech more to himself than to the woman. That was how he was. He worked out all his things inside himself, as if it were all merely an interior problem of his own. And while he did so, he had an odd way of squinting his left eye and wagging his head loosely, like a man talking absolutely to himself, and turning his eyes inwards. (III, 613)

He can't look straight at her. It is a gamble 'in which he could not lose desperately' (III, 612), it excites him. She can and perhaps will lose desperately in it. For him it's an idea – pretty soon he throws in her child as well. Let them both come and live with him! And having met and had some conversation with her husband, it becomes a fight with him, the woman as a token – that is what really excites him. 'It was not that he was in *love* with the woman. But, my God, he wanted to take her away from that man' (III, 624). When despite his own doubts and his urging her to think again, she arrives at Marylebone Station with her daughter, he excites himself with thoughts of defeating, in her, the man she has just left, her husband.

The miner has his own complaint, which he makes to Jimmy with force and clarity: "'I'm nothing but made use of,'" he said [...] "Down the pit, I'm made use of, and they give me a wage, such as it is. At the house I'm made use of, and my wife sets the dinner on the table as if I was a customer in a shop.'" He says these words 'hard and final to himself, and staring into space'; but this is an introspection, unlike Jimmy's, which has resulted in a view he will hold to, to change his life. He challenges Jimmy with it: 'he turned and looked straight and hard into Jimmy's eyes' (III, 620). He views him and his sudden desire to carry off wife and child with incredulity and amused contempt, and then, most damningly, as the convenient means by which he may attain to a freedom of his own. He says: "'I look on you as an instument [...] Something had to break. You are the instrument that breaks it'" (III, 626).

It is a bitter story. The woman, unhappy in her marriage, contributes to her husband's sense of being merely an object. He himself, rather like Jimmy, wants another sort of woman, one who will please him and will want to please him, as he says; and he has found such a person outside his marriage who will serve for now. And Jimmy's view of life in a colliery village as 'the real stuff' is valid, at least in the contrast with his own factitiousness. He is annulled by the (however unhappy) intimacy of the miner and his wife and by their rituals – the man's return from the pit, the washing, the meal. His interest in Emilia when she risks herself and her daughter into his life, is essentially only vengeful, against the man she is 'hopelessly married to' (III, 629).

Fiction is a means to a truer consciousness of our real situation. The writer of stories and poems strives sentence by sentence, line by line, to cleave to the truth of them. The truth of a story or a poem is not the same as the factual accuracy of a parliamentary report or the honest assessment, say by a social worker, of a person's situation and prospects. Jimmy is not John Middleton Murry, he is a fictional character whom we can learn from if we attend to him, in the story, as closely and critically as his author did.

CONCLUSION

It is a matter of life and death in Lawrence's stories: the struggle for a life you can call your own, the living death if you refuse the struggle or fail in it. He asks of his characters that they become conscious of the realities of their situation – not only their material circumstances but also their own just demands in those circumstances, the demands they must raise and assert if they are to live more honestly. Lawrence thought this necessary struggle to be a national as well as an individual and personal matter. He thought that the nation – indeed much of humanity – was living untruthfully, not facing up to the facts of modernity (at their worst in the War). For very survival, people, as individuals and as citizens of the state, need to live in the consciousness of what life *now* is like. But fiction can't deal with a nation, let alone with the race; it has to deal with particulars. So Lawrence's stories show individuals struggling (or refusing to struggle) to live truthfully. Art can only work like that. And in practice, of course, any larger regeneration – towards a less dishonest society – can only begin in those moments when individual men and women refuse the pervasive lying and evasion (and the oppression they entail) and demand the truth and the freedom to live *in* truth.

DAVID CONSTANTINE

Ten Essential Stories

'The Prussian Officer' (1913)★
'The Thorn in the Flesh' (1914)
'Daughters of the Vicar' (1911)★
'The Shades of Spring' (1914)
'Odour of Chrysanthemums' (1911)★
'The Blind Man' (1921)
'You Touched Me' (1921)
'The Horse-dealer's Daughter' (1922)★
'Jimmy and the desperate Woman' (1924)★
'The Man who loved Islands' (1927)

Alison MacLeod

on

Katherine Mansfield

I

At last, that moment – 'I wrote and finished a story yesterday [...] one feels like a leaf on the ground – one can't even flutter. At the same time there is a feeling of joy that another story is finished.' (Murry 1941: 438)

ON NEW YEAR'S Day, 1921, two years before her death, Katherine Mansfield wrote to her brother-in-law, the artist Richard Murry: 'I have written a huge long story of a rather new kind [...] It's a queer tale, though. I hope you'll like it' (Murry 1941: 359). Her queer tale was 'The Daughters of the Late Colonel', the story of Constantia and Josephine, two unmarried sisters who have known little more than their father's barked orders and the thumped commands of his walking stick. Life 'had been looking after Father and at the same time keeping out of Father's way.' But now, Father is dead, and the sisters, timid and tentative after a lifetime of his rule, must not only plan his funeral and parcel up his things, they must persuade themselves that he is *gone*.

As the story opens, it is a week since his death, and yet the 'Late Colonel' seems to refuse to die.

What would Father say when he found out? For he was bound to find out sooner or later. He always did. 'Buried. You two girls had me *buried*!' [...] Oh, what would they say? What possible excuse could they make? It sounded such an apparently heartless thing to do [...] And the expense, she thought, stepping into the tight-buttoned cab. When she had to show him the bills. What would he say then?

She heard him absolutely roaring. 'And do you expect me to pay for this gimcrack excursion of yours?' (Mansfield 2007: 268-269)

Like all great stories, 'The Daughters of the Late Colonel' springs from a pivotal moment of change. The *pater familias* is dead and nothing will ever be entirely familiar again. In his final moments, the sisters received neither fatherly blessing nor the peace of a deathbed scene, and now, they are haunted by his final burst of life:

...as they were standing there, wondering what to do, he had suddenly opened one eye. Oh, what a difference to their memory of him, how much easier to tell people about it, if he had only opened both! But no – one eye only. It had glared at them for a moment and then [...] went out. (Mansfield 2007: 266-267)

Here, and in other Mansfield stories, meaning is kindled by the 'narrative friction' of two elements that tug against one another . In 'The Daughters', the forces of life and death are at odds; the ordinary see-saws into the extraordinary and back again. An eye that should have remained shut has opened unnaturally. It is a contrary eye, and the tension suspended in contradictions often fuels great short fiction. A lesser writer would have been satisfied with the more standard observation of both eyes flashing open moments before the death. But Mansfield's own eye is thrillingly precise, and she offers us the inspired oddity – so odd it feels instantly true – of the Colonel's one avid, glaring eye.

Virginia Woolf 'adored' Mansfield's 'sharpness and reality' (Tomalin 1987: 204). For Leonard Woolf, she was an 'intense realist' (Tomalin 1987: 184). But does that description capture Mansfield's peculiar gift? In detail after sharply etched detail, in story after story, she achieves something more vivid than even a heightened verisimilitude; she creates stories that are powerfully visceral and, with that, weirdly 'animate'. When the Colonel's eye opens, we draw breath. We almost jump back.

The same precision of focus animates – strangely and audaciously – the final lines of such stories as 'Miss Brill' and 'The Doll's House'. It's an effect that few story writers achieve and yet it is the short story form at its most remarkable, its most alive. At their best, Mansfield's stories are kinetic. 'Do you, too,' asks Mansfield, 'feel an infinite delight and value in *detail* – not for the sake of detail but for the life *in* the life of it? I can never express myself…' (Murry 1941: 27). For Mansfield, a successful book is 'a living book. What I mean by that is, it is warm; one can put it down and it goes on breathing' (Murry 1941: 417).

In the sisters' world, life – released at last from the tyranny of the Colonel's stick – grows unpredictable, and Mansfield's finely observed realism tips into the surreal. The family's porter inherits the Colonel's top-hat, and the sisters 'see' his head 'disappearing' and then popping out 'like a candle'. Connie and Jug's 'spy' of a housekeeper tends to burst in upon them, 'as though she had discovered some secret panel in the wall.' For pudding, she serves the sisters 'a white, terrified blancmange.' When Cyril, their nephew visits, there is an absurdly insistent conversation about – meringues. And when the daughters finally manage to enter the Colonel's vacant bedroom, the Colonel, they discover, has not vacated the premises. He clings stubbornly on.

'And why do you keep on staring at the bed?' said Josephine, raising her voice almost defiantly. 'There's nothing *on* the bed.'

'Oh, Jug, don't say so!' said poor Connie. 'At any rate, not so loudly.' […]

Josephine could only glare. She had the most extraordinary feeling that she had just escaped something simply awful. But how could she explain to Constantia that Father was in the chest of drawers? He was in the top drawer with his handkerchiefs and neckties, or in the next with his shirts and pyjamas, or in the lowest of all with his suits. He was watching there, hidden away – just behind the door-handle – ready to spring. (Mansfield 2007: 271)

When his whereabouts are, at last, confirmed as the wardrobe – and when Josephine turns the key, locking away the bullying phantom of their father – absurd though it may be, we feel the full force of her triumph.

In Mansfield, the physical world is endlessly plastic. A head may also be a candle. A blancmange may exhibit fear. A dead father may be in a top drawer. Mansfield, stooped with rheumatism, describes herself as a 'permanent croquet hoop' (Murry 1941: 67). For her, a chill, foggy day in October is 'living inside a pearl' (Murry 1941: 223). On a mantelpiece in her host's dining room, Mansfield spots 'a big corpse of a clock' (Murry 1941: 358). When she meets John Middleton Murry, her husband-to-be, she noted his 'lovely, frightening mouth' (Tomalin 1987: 96). In her prose phrasing, she often yokes the disparate into fresh, dynamic images.

Of her own writing process she says, 'I feel as fastidious as though I wrote with acid' (Murry 1941: 4). She is also 'a powerful stickler for form' (Murry 1941: 4): 'I mean down to details […] I choose not only the length of every sentence, but even the sound of every sentence. I choose the rise and fall of every paragraph […] I read it aloud – numbers of times – just as one would play over a musical composition – trying to get it nearer and nearer […] If a thing has really come off it seems to me there mustn't be one single word out of place, or one word that could be taken out' (Murry 1941: 360-61).

Mansfield was among the first English-speaking readers to experience the radically new stories of Anton Chekhov, who had died of tuberculosis in 1904, nine years before she was to discover him. Mansfield herself would fall ill with the disease in 1910 and would die of it in 1923. (She writes: 'My cough is so much worse that I *am* a cough – a living, walking or lying down cough,' Murry 1941: 502.) She felt a passionate affinity with Chekhov, Chekhov's stories and his technique. 'Ach, Tchekhov! Why are you dead? Why can't I talk to you – in a big, darkish room – at late evening – where the light is green from the waving trees outside. I'd like to write a series of *Heavens*: that would be one' (Scott 2002: #12, 141). If she could write a series of 'Heavens', it was perhaps because she couldn't bring herself to believe in one: 'we've only one life and I cannot believe in immortality. I wish I could' (Murry 1941: 195).

From Chekhov, she inherited an understanding of the short story as a form that can re-create an experience of life's flux. Her stories 'plunge' us in. 'The week after…' begins 'The Daughters'. 'Very early morning' opens her story 'At the Bay'. 'And after all…' starts 'The Garden Party'. Each story is already in motion as we join it – as any real world is.

Each also ends on a note not so much of *ambiguity* – that word doesn't do justice to the best of Mansfield's endings – but at a point where the characters' (and our) 'knowing' is inseparable from an 'unknowing'; where revelation is bound by mystery. One is not more true than the other. Perhaps even more so than in the stories of Chekhov, we arrive at the suggestion of an *abundant* provisionality. In Mansfield's fluxing conclusions, her aim is not the avoidance, suspension or deferral of meaning, but rather a meaning that 'has' an aftermath, a meaning with an 'afterlife' even – in other words, meaning *in motion*. To Virginia Woolf, she suggests that 'what the writer does is not so much to solve the question but to put the question. There must be the question put' (Murry 1941: 204).

Like her fellow modernists, Mansfield was interested in the slipstream of human consciousness, although I'd suggest she was influenced less by her peers (D.H. Lawrence, Virginia Woolf, James Joyce) than – again – by Chekhov, whose innovations in the rendering of thought and inner life we find in stories like 'Ward 6'. Here is his character Dr. Ragin, in his final moments of life: 'A herd of deer, extraordinarily beautiful and graceful [...] raced past him; then a peasant woman stretched out a hand to him with a registered letter [...] The postmaster said something.' (Chekhov 2002: 186). In Mansfield's 'The Daughters of the Late Colonel', during an evening meal, Constantia gazes away 'far over the desert, to where that line of camels unwound like a thread of wool'. Later, as they imagine sending their father's watch to their brother in Ceylon, both sisters pause 'to watch a black man in white linen drawers running through the pale fields for dear life, with a large brown-paper parcel in his hands. Josephine's black man was tiny [...] like an ant. But there was something blind and tireless about Constantia's tall, thin fellow.'

'The Daughters of the Late Colonel' was Mansfield's only story that satisfied her 'to any extent' (Murry 1941: 444), but she was disappointed and perplexed by the response from reviewers and readers: 'I put my all into that story and hardly anyone saw what I was getting at. Even dear old Hardy told me to write more about those sisters. As if there was any more to say!' (Murry 1941: 414). Her readers thought the story 'cruel'; 'they thought I was "sneering" at Jug and Constantia; or they thought it was "drab" [...] It's almost terrifying to be misunderstood' (Murry 1941: 389).

Mansfield believed that 'tenderness' was a quality that defined the best of literature (Murry 1941: 434 and 447). 'There was a moment when I first had "the idea" when I saw the two sisters as *amusing;* but the moment I looked deeper (let me be quite frank) I bowed down to the beauty that was hidden in their lives…' (Murry 1941: 389).

What beauty? you might wonder. 'To live, to live!' is a longing expressed or felt by many a Chekhov character, and a painful but sometimes exquisite yearning *towards life* is also fundamental to Mansfield's outlook and her mature work. 'To live – to live – that is all – and to leave Life on this earth as Tchekhov left life' (Scott 2002: Unbound, 202). In Mansfield, this yearning, often driven by a character's isolation or loneliness, is simply but powerfully evoked. After Chekhov and Mansfield, it's arguable that longing or yearning becomes *the* vital dynamic in the modern short story form.

By the conclusion of 'The Daughters of the Late Colonel', Mansfield is approaching the 'hidden country' of the 'new' type of prose fiction (Murry 1941: 210) that was her early ambition to write. Here is a prose that captures, minutely, the details of the external world, not for the sake of it, but to reveal, like a flare over dark water, the mystery of our inner lives. At the end of 'The Daughters', the essence of Connie – the 'Connie-ness' of Connie, the 'beauty' of her inner life and longing – suddenly flickers, alive, tender and surprising, on the page:

> There had been this other life, running out, bringing things home in bags, getting things on approval, discussing them with Jug, and taking them back to get more things on approval, and arranging Father's trays and trying not to annoy Father. But it all seemed to have happened in a kind of tunnel. It wasn't real. It was only when she came out of the tunnel into the moonlight or by the sea or into a thunderstorm that she really felt herself. What did it mean? What was it she was always wanting? (Mansfield 2007: 184)

'I confess,' Mansfield writes, ' I only feel that I'm doing right when I am living by love. I don't mean a personal love – you know – but – the big thing. Why should one love? No reason;

it's just a mystery. But it is like light. I can only truly see things in its rays.' (Murry 1941: 299)

In each one of her stories, she draws upon an almost painterly love of colour, the natural elements, and the play of light. At the end of 'The Daughters', 'Josephine, too, forgot to be practical and sensible; she smiled faintly, strangely. On the Indian carpet there fell a square of sunlight, pale red; it came and went and came – and stayed, deepened – until it shone almost golden. "The sun's out," said Josephine, as though it really mattered.'

In these moments – Josephine in the light, Constantia remembering herself in the open air – we know the daughters for who they actually are, and 'real' life flares on the page. That is the story writer's art and gift – the gift of a *felt* experience of life.

Mansfield was inspired by the paintings of the Post-Impressionists, and particularly by Van Gogh: 'They taught me something about writing, which was queer, a kind of freedom, or rather, a shaking free.' (Murry 1941: 423) In 1921, at her most mature stage of writing and working at full tilt against her approaching death, her sense of form loses the brittleness that sometimes weakened her earlier work, and the overly determined formal effects we see in such stories as her (nevertheless wonderful) 1920 story 'Prelude', with its self-consciously abrupt transitions. Her craft is also free of the over insistent symbolism of later hard-working stories, like her 1922 story 'The Fly' ['I hated writing it,' Murry 1941: 473].

As she writes 'The Daughters', Mansfield's style is as economic and sharp as ever, but the lines of her composition are growing more fluid, more supple. Of the structure of 'The Daughters', she tells Richard Murry, 'it just unfolds and opens' (Murry 1941: 359). Her sense of form is organic. Her choice of verbs suggests a 'flowering', for the opening of 'The Daughters' both holds and hides the seed of its own ending.

She is by this time very conscious of her own ending: 'The only occasion when I ever felt leisure [...] was while writing The Daughters of the Late Col. And then at the end I was so terribly unhappy that I wrote as fast as possible for fear of dying before the story was sent.' (Scott 2002: #20, 318)

II.

In September 1921, Mansfield wrote to her artist friend Dorothy Brett: 'I've just finished my new book. Finished last night at 10:30. Laid down the pen after writing "Thanks be to God." I wish there was a God. I am longing to (1) praise him, (2) thank him. The title is *At the Bay*. That's the name of a very long story in it – a continuation of *Prelude*. [...] I've been at it all night. [...] It's as good as I can do, and all my heart and soul is in it [...] every single bit.' (Murry 1941: 400)

'At the Bay' is the story of the Burnells, an extended family who are summering in one of the bungalows that nestle close to Crescent Bay. Here we discover characters whom we have already met in Mansfield's 'New Zealand stories' like 'Prelude' and 'The Doll's House', and new faces too. We enter the lives of Linda and Stanley Burnell, Linda's sister Beryl, Linda's mother Mrs Fairfield, and the children – Isabel, Kezia and Lottie – as well as Alice, their domestic help, and the Burnells's relations the Trouts: father Jonathan and his boys, Rags and Pip. We see, too, the Kembers, the mysterious couple who have been much noticed in the summer colony of the Bay.

The action unfolds over a single day and across almost 60 pages. We join the story on the cusp of the new day, when the world of the Bay is still veiled:

Very early morning. The sun was not yet risen, and the whole of Crescent Bay was hidden under a white sea-mist. The big bush-covered hills at the back were smothered. You could not see where they ended and the paddocks and bungalows began. The sandy road was gone and the paddocks and bungalows either side of it; there were no white dunes covered with reddish grass beyond them; there was nothing to mark which was the beach and where was the sea. (Mansfield 2007: 205)

Mansfield's attention to 'hidden-ness' at the outset is everything. The story's plot structure is not the standard, forward-moving composition in which one scene gives way inexorably (or incidentally) to the next, but rather, a 'lifting of the mist' – a quiet revelation of hidden truths – in episode after distinct episode.

In Part I, as the sun rises and burns off the mist, the hidden elements of the Bay are revealed. The secret strangeness of the landscape reverts to the familiar. 'It looked as though the sea had beaten up softly in the darkness [...] Perhaps if you'd waked up in the middle of the night you might have seen a big fish flicking in at the window and gone again.' Elsewhere in the summer colony, a shock-haired giant turns back into the big gum tree outside Mrs. Stubbs's shop. A pattering flock of sheep emerge from around the corner. We hear the whistling of the shepherd 'mournful and tender'. Telegraph poles flash 'into points of light'.

In Parts II and III, we watch Stanley and Jonathan at their early morning bathe in the sea before work. As the narrative veil lifts, we glimpse the private dissatisfaction of each family man. Jonathan is inclined to chat. Stanley is not: 'I want to get this over. I'm in a hurry. I've work to do this morning – see?' The presence of Jonathan spoils his bathe. Jonathan has very different concerns as he is lifted briefly on a powerful wave. 'And now there came another. That was the way to live – carelessly, recklessly, spending oneself [...] To live—to live! [...] And stalking up the beach, shivering, all his muscles tight, he too felt his bathe was spoilt. He'd stayed in too long.' Back at home, Stanley's wife and family look forward only to the moment he will have left for the day. 'Oh, the relief, the difference it made to have the man out of the house. Their very voices changed as they called to one another; they sounded warm and loving and as if they shared a secret.' In Mansfield, loving relationships are often sharply ambivalent.

In Part IV, the children dig up secret treasure on the beach. These secrets foreshadow others to come. '"Promise not to tell,"' insists Pip to his cousins as he opens his hand… Mansfield has a remarkable gift for capturing a child's point of view – a gift she sometimes uses, wilfully and almost eccentrically, to evoke the points of view of animals as well. In a review written approximately six months before she began 'At the Bay', she reasons:

> And therefore the childhood that we look back upon and attempt to recreate must be – if it is to satisfy our longing as well as our memory – a great deal more than a catalogue of infant pleasures and pangs. It must have, as it were, a haunting light upon it. (Scott 2002: Intro, xxii)

This 'haunting light' glimmers not only in 'At the Bay', but in several other stories, like 'The Doll's House', in which an actual lamp, one that is both ordinary and discomforting, closes the story.

In Part V, amid the dunes and the heaps of clothes and the 'whiskery' waves, the mystery of the Kembers emerges, but obliquely, as if not by authorial design. Seemingly random, ordinary moments give way to the remarkable appearance of Mrs Kember: 'She was the only woman at the Bay who smoked […] The women at the Bay thought she was very, very fast […] Mrs. Kember's husband was at least ten years younger than she was, and so incredibly handsome that he looked like a mask […] he ignored his wife just as she ignored him. How did he live?' On a more remote part of the beach, Mrs Kember will openly flirt with Beryl: '"Why be shy? I shan't eat you [...] Really, it's a sin for you to wear clothes, my dear.'" In a disconcerting moment for Beryl in the water, Mrs Kember's face surfaces, and suddenly, perversely, she resembles her husband.

In Part VI, we stumble upon another private moment that is, once again, at apparent odds with the picturesque idyll of the Bay. Relaxing in the garden of their bungalow, Linda reflects on her love for her husband Stanley: 'not the everyday one, but a timid, sensitive, innocent Stanley [...] who longed to be good.' The tenderness of the moment makes the following revelation even more stark to the reader: 'what was left of her time was spent in dread of having children [...] She was broken, made weak, her courage was gone, through child-bearing. And what made it doubly hard to bear was, she did not love her children,' a truth she tells her little son in a detached way as he smiles up at her. The moment is shocking, even over 90 years since the lines were written. Mansfield is a bold writer and does not rest with comfortable or more palatable half-truths. In 'At the Bay', as in stories like 'Bliss' and 'Je Ne Parle Pas Francais', her characters break taboos while their author declines to pass judgement upon them – another Chekhovian legacy. In his own time, Chekhov was attacked as 'the high-priest of unprincipled writing'. Yet, like Chekhov, Mansfield's aim is not to scandalize her reader, but rather to be as true to life as her talents allow.

In Part VII, during the peace of their afternoon nap, little Kezia learns from her grandmother that, one day, everyone will die, and she is shocked: 'She didn't want to die. It meant she would have to leave here, leave everywhere, for ever.' Mansfield's own fear of death finds expression in the scene, and in other stories of the period ('The Daughters of the Late Colonel', 'The Garden Party', 'Prelude', 'The Fly'). Indeed, the tragedy of her short life (she died at 34) seems strangely matched to a form that, in its brevity and compression, has become a perfect crucible for narratives of life's intensities, including death.

And so 'At The Bay' unfolds, episode after episode, secret by secret. The servant-girl Alice ventures out for a secret tea. The children play cards in a shed in a darkening world of their own. The day fades. Jonathan arrives to collect his children. Linda, his sister-in-law, privately notes 'how attractive he [is].' Yet, for all his good cheer, she knows that he goes 'about with a look like hunger in his black eyes'. Jonathan is trapped in the life of 'an ordinary clerk' and imagines himself as '"an insect that's flown into the room of its own accord. I dash against the walls, dash against the windows [...] And all the while I'm thinking [...] "The shortness of life! The shortness of life!"'

In the final episode, Beryl has a mystery assignation – with, we realise, the dark and ambiguous figure of Mr Kember. Nothing has foreshadowed their relationship to this point, except perhaps Beryl's confused blurring of Mr and Mrs Kember in the earlier scene on the beach. '"Frightened?"' he mocks her now at her window. '"Not in the least," said she. As she spoke that weak thing within her seemed to uncoil, to grow tremendously strong; she longed to go!'

In 'At the Bay', there is no 'building' of narrative tension across a unity of scenes; instead Mansfield relies on a strong revelatory dynamic; on an episode-by-episode unveiling. Truths are brought into sunlight; the forbidden is risked; secrets are given up. By the story's end, it is late, and the reader, too, is briefly implicated: 'everything, even the bedpost, knows you, responds, shares your secret.' Yet in Mansfield, even secret knowledge and divided lives cannot divide the world – or her artistic vision.

We return to the landscape of Crescent Bay in the final paragraphs of the story. A 'serene' cloud passes over the moon. The sea sounds briefly troubled. Then the cloud sails away, the sea 'wakes out of a dark dream', and 'all was still'. There is a quietly visionary sense at work in Mansfield's mature work, a sense that reality – like the dawn mist and the stones on the beach and the shore itself – is 'porous' (a favourite adjective for Mansfield in 'At the Bay'). Division is an illusion. All is secretly one.

Commenting on 'The Garden Party', which she started in October 1921, soon after completing 'At The Bay', Mansfield writes: '[Laura] feels things ought to happen differently. First one and then another. But life isn't like that. We haven't the ordering of it. Laura says, "But all these things [a garden party, a man dead in the road] must not happen at once." *And Life answers, "Why not? How are they divided from each other?"* [my emphasis]' (Murry 1941: 454)

Mansfield often describes her 'philosophy', in life and in her writing, as 'the defeat of the personal' (e.g. Scott 2002: #22, 190). 'One must,' she writes, 'learn, one must practise to forget oneself. I can't tell the truth about Aunt Anne unless I am free to enter into her life without self-consciousness.' (Scott 2002: #41, 296) 'I sometimes wonder whether the act of surrender is not one of the greatest of all – the highest. It is one of the (most) difficult of all [...] You see it's so immensely complicated. It "needs" real humility and at the same time an absolute belief in one's own essential freedom. It is an act of faith. [...] like all great acts it is *pure risk*. This is true for me as a human being and as a writer.' (Murry 1941: 351)

She tries to describe that act of 'surrender': 'When I write about ducks I swear that I am a white duck with a round eye, floating on a pond [...] In fact the whole process of becoming the duck [...] is so thrilling that I can hardly breathe, only to think about it. For although that is as far as most people can get, it is really only the "prelude". There follows the moment when you are *more* duck, *more* apple, or *more* Natasha than any of these objects could ever possibly be, and so you *create* them anew' (Murry 1941: 474). 'I've been this man, been this woman. I've stood for hours on the Auckland Wharf. I've been out in the stream waiting to be berthed – I've been a seagull hovering at the stern and a hotel porter whistling through his teeth. It isn't as though one sits and watches the spectacle. That would be thrilling enough, God knows. But one is the spectacle for the time.' (Murry 1941: 347)

This imaginative process is crucial to both her art and her technique: 'that is why I believe in technique, too [...] I don't see how art is going to make that divine *spring* into the bounding outline of things if it hasn't passed through the process of trying to become these things before re-creating them.' (Murry 1941: 396) For Mansfield, the making of stories is an experience of 'possession', a word she often uses in her letters and notebooks: 'I mean the moment when the act of creation takes place – the mysterious change – when you are no longer writing the book, *it* is writing, *it* possesses you.' (Murry 1941: 338)

Throughout her fiction, her diaries and notebooks, the natural world is lovingly and minutely evoked. Trees, flowers and birds are always specified. The focus she achieves in these descriptions is often so precise, so 'alive', the experience of reading her work is almost uncanny. She writes to Richard Murry: 'Oh, Richard – I do love the earth! When I go off by myself here – one slips through the tree trunks and one is out of sight at once – hidden from every eye. That's my joy. [... My] only trouble is that I can't make some small grasshoppery sound now and then.' (Murry 1941: 396). She is frequently dismissive of 'that dreadful glaze of "intellectuality"' (Murry 1941: 479) in the fiction she is being sent to review. 'But warm, eager living life – to be rooted in life… That is what I want. And nothing less.' (Scott 2002: #30, 287)

In June 1921, as she began 'At the Bay', she wrote: 'I must [...] get on with my new story. It's called "At the Bay" and it's (I hope) full of sand and seaweed, bathing dresses hanging over verandas, and sandshoes on window sills, and little pink "sea" convolvulus, and rather gritty sandwiches and the tide coming in. And it smells (oh I *do* hope it smells) a little bit fishy' (Murry 1941: 394). It was her 'seaweedy story' (Murry 1941: 408). But these accounts don't capture the importance of 'thinginess' to Mansfield's technique: 'I like always to have a great grasp of Life, so that I intensify the so-called small things – so that truly everything is significant.'

(O'Sullivan 1984: I, 88) Later she recalls: 'It took me nearly a month to recover from "At the Bay". I could not get away from the sound of the sea and Beryl fanning her hair at the window. These things would not die down.' (Scott 2002: #31, 291)

Her compelling attention to the things and details of the world means she is often described as a 'miniaturist', a maker of delicate, precise and often ephemeral things. But the word doesn't do justice to the force of her work: 'You see I too have a passion for technique. I have a passion for making the thing into a *whole*' (Murry 1941: 364). Indeed, Mansfield's literary technique and artistic vision is a hard-won, high-risk commitment to what she termed 'a visionary consciousness.' (Murry 1941: 387)

She describes the achievement of the 'visionary' mind by turning once more to her literary hero's achievement: 'as in the stories of Chekhov, we should become aware of the rain pattering on the roof all night long, of the languid, feverish wind, of the moonlit orchard and the first snow, passionately realized, not indeed as analogous to a state of mind, but as linking that mind to the larger whole' (Mansfield 1930, 54). Yet the joy she experienced upon the completion of a story rarely lasted. 'As I re-read "At the Bay" in proof it seemed to me flat, dull, and not a success at all. I was very much ashamed of it. I am. But now to resolve! And especially to keep in touch with life.'

Life was all. Mansfield, as I note above, did not believe in a personal God or a Christian afterlife. Of her writing she said, 'It [...] *is* my religion – of people – of "life" – it is life' (Scott 2002: #16, 168). Even her darker stories, 'like 'The Daughters of the Late Colonel', are defiant acts of praise. 'You know,' she writes, 'how when one woman carries the new born baby the other woman approaches and says "Bless it." But I am always wanting to lift the handkerchief off lizards' faces and pansies' faces and the house by moonlight. I'm always wanting to *put a blessing* on what I see. It's a queer feeling.' (Murry 1941: 327-28)

Ten Essential Stories

'Bliss' (1918)
'Prelude' (1918)
'Miss Brill' (1920)
'The Daughters of the Late Colonel' (1921)★
'Her First Ball' (1921)
'The Voyage' (1921)
'At the Bay' (1922)★
'The Doll's House' (1922)
'The Fly' (1922)
'The Garden Party' (1922)

Ramsey Campbell

on

H.P. Lovecraft

THE FATHERS OF the modern horror story are Poe in America and Le Fanu in Britain, both of whom refined Gothic methods to produce seminal stories in the field. Nor should Hoffmann's psychological fantasies be overlooked. If I take Lovecraft to be the most important single twentieth-century writer of tales of terror, it's because he unites the traditions that preceded him on both sides of the Atlantic and builds on their strengths. His *Supernatural Horror in Literature* is not only an appreciation of all that he found best in the genre and a critique of the flaws he saw, but also a statement of his own artistic ambitions. His fiction gives them life.

To an extent his reputation is the victim of his most famous creation, the Lovecraft Mythos. This took very gradual shape throughout most of his career, and involves inhuman beings from outer space or from other dimensions, creatures that are indifferent to man but often worshipped as gods or occult forces. He often cited references to them from the *Necronomicon*, his invented tome that took on such a life of its own that several versions by later writers have been published. The Mythos was conceived as an antidote to conventional Victorian occultism – as an attempt to reclaim the imaginative appeal of the unknown – and is only one of many ways his tales suggest worse, or greater, than they show. It is also just one of his means of reaching for a sense of wonder, the aim that produces the visionary horror of his finest work (by no means all of it belonging to the Mythos). His stories represent a search for the perfect form for the weird tale, a process in which he tried out all the forms and all the styles of prose he could.

Nevertheless the Mythos is his most visible bequest to the field, because it looks so easy to imitate or draw upon. As one of the first writers to copy Lovecraft without having known him, I must take some of the blame for the way his concept has been rendered over-explicit and over-explained, precisely the reverse of his intentions. Luckily his influence is far more profound. In his essays and letters he was able to preserve the notion of horror fiction as literature despite all the assaults pulp writing had made on its best qualities, a view that was especially fruitful in the case of Fritz Leiber, who followed his mentor's example of uniting the transatlantic traditions. Other correspondents such as Robert Bloch, Donald Wandrei and Henry Kuttner assimilated his vision into their own. More recently such diverse talents as T. E. D. Klein, Thomas Ligotti and Poppy Z. Brite have acknowledged Lovecraft's importance to their work, but who could accuse any of them of simple mimicry? His use of suggestion and allusion might seem beyond the reach of most filmmakers, but I submit *The Blair Witch Project* as the key Lovecraftian film, not least in the documentary realism he urged upon serious artists in the field and in the inexplicitness with which it conveys, to use his phrase, dread suspense.

Yet Lovecraft's achievement lies not so much in his influence as in the enduring qualities of his finest work. The field would be all the richer if more writers learned from both his care for structure and his larger principles. His yearning for the cosmic is the greatest strength of his best tales. He is one of the few masters of the tale of terror that reaches for, and often attains, awe. I'm going to examine in some detail the structures and use of language that he employed to this and other ends.

I want to start by looking at his earliest recognisably personal story, 'Dagon'. This was written in July 1917, and applies the principles he admired in Poe's tales of supernatural horror: 'the maintenance of a single mood and achievement of a single impression in a tale, and the rigorous paring down of incidents to such as have a direct bearing on the plot and will figure prominently in the climax.' (Lovecraft 1986: 396). Lovecraft wrote this in *Supernatural Horror in Literature*, where he analyses Poe's 'The Fall of the House of Usher' as demonstrating 'the essential details to emphasise, the precise incongruities and conceits to select as preliminaries or concomitants to horror, the exact incidents and allusions to throw out innocently in advance as symbols or prefigurings of each major step toward the hideous dénouement to come, the nice adjustments of cumulative force and the unerring accuracy in linkage of parts which make for faultless unity throughout and thunderous effectiveness at the climactic moment, the delicate nuances of scenic and landscape value to select in establishing and sustaining the desired mood and vitalising the desired illusion.' (Lovecraft 1986: 399) It's worth remarking that when a writer analyses someone else's work they are often also talking about their own, and we shall see how he developed these methods in his own fiction.

August Derleth – prime mover of Arkham House, Lovecraft's first hardcover publisher – once summed up Lovecraft's structure thus: 'Lovecraft got his effects by beginning soberly and with restraint, being careful to link his stories to reality, and proceeded with them with an air of doubt, as if the facts he chronicled could not mean what they did, so that the ultimate effect was all the more damning...' (Letter to myself; Campbell 2011: 294). We may observe that the opening tone is often restrained even when the material is Gothic; like Poe, Lovecraft was refining elements of the Gothic novel, focusing more closely on psychology and the supernatural. So 'Dagon' opens with the lines 'I am writing this under an appreciable mental strain, since by tonight I shall be no more. Penniless, and at the end of my supply of the drug which alone makes life endurable, I can bear the torture no longer; and shall cast myself from this garret window into the squalid street below' (Lovecraft 2002a: 1). While this is undoubtedly melodramatic, it serves to warn the reader to examine the narrator's tale carefully, since it may be to some extent delusional. The unreliable narrator is a favourite and certainly effective device of the genre, enriching many tales since Poe's 'Tell-tale Heart' with ambiguity. It often means that the tale can be interpreted psychologically without losing its uncanny dimension. Sometimes (as in *Rosemary's Baby*, which can certainly be read as a study of prenatal paranoia) restricting the reader's view to a single consciousness works just as well.

Having established the background to the narrator's situation in just three paragraphs, Lovecraft immediately immerses us in it. 'The change happened while I slept...' Like quite a few of his stories, 'Dagon' is based on a nightmare and seems designed to convey the intensity of that experience. The sense of dislocation – of finding yourself somewhere you have no memory of reaching – will recur in later tales; it's surely a powerful symbol of psychological breakdown. The paragraphs describing the upheaved landscape recall the opening of Poe's 'Usher' (itself an object lesson in setting the scene) in their oppressive vividness. Besides painting the scene in words, Lovecraft uses sound (or rather its absence) and smell to render it more immediate. There's also an early use of a technique that his detractors often seize upon – inexplicitness as a means of stimulating the reader's imagination. Here the reference to 'other less describable things' that infest the mud is surely appropriate, implying that they're the remains of creatures carried up from depths so profound that the narrator can't identify the species (which a later reference suggests is prehistoric). At the same time the phrase seems intended to evoke disquiet, and it works that way for me.

The paragraphs describing the narrator's trek and its destination exemplify a style of prose Lovecraft often writes: realistic in detail – documentary, if you like – and yet incantatory in its choice of language. At times the language rises to a crescendo that includes poetic usages ('I know not why my dreams were so wild that night; but ere the waning and fantastically gibbous moon had risen far above the eastern plain, I was awake in a cold perspiration, determined to sleep no more' (Lovecraft 2002a: 3)) but just as important to its effect are the modulations that lead up to the linguistic climaxes, best represented by the paragraph that describes the pictorial carvings on the monolith. A rare lurch into cliché ('Then suddenly I saw it') betrays that this is an early tale. The story ends with what can only be a hallucination, which throws the rest of the narrative into question but doesn't, I think, lessen the power of its vision. That this vision meant a good deal to Lovecraft is clear from its recurrence and elaboration in his later work.

When writing horror it's important to be aware of the difference between this genre and that of magic realism. In 'Notes on Writing Weird Fiction' (1937) Lovecraft writes 'Never have a wonder taken for granted. Even when the characters are supposed to be accustomed to the wonder I try to weave an air of awe and impressiveness corresponding to what the reader should feel […] Atmosphere, not action, is the great desideratum of weird fiction. Indeed, all that a wonder story can ever be is *a vivid picture of a certain type of human mood.*' (Lovecraft 1995: 116)

It's worth noting that in 'Dagon' the narrator is entirely uncharacterised except by his behaviour; we never even learn what he was doing on the ship that was captured. There need be nothing wrong with this. Writers as different as Poe, Kafka and Samuel Beckett have conveyed terror by describing only a narrator's experiences, using them to illuminate his psychology. The American writer Steve Rasnic Tem has observed that the protagonist in a third-person tale of terror tends to be represented by a pronoun once they have been identified by name, so that they don't intervene too much between the narrative and our reading of their direct experience. In his essay 'One View: Creating Character in

Fantasy and Horror Fiction' Tem writes 'all other objects in the story – the landscape, the other characters, the supernatural presence, even the individual events – represent some aspect of the protagonist (or victim).' (Tem 1987: 37).

In 'The Rats in the Walls' (written in August-September 1923) Lovecraft applies his documentary method to character, although the opening paragraphs are equally a chronicle of the location and an account of the tales told about it. By conflating these and the ancestry of the narrator he suggests how (again echoing Poe's 'Usher') the place and its inhabitants share a common occult identity. It's also worth noting that the very first phrase establishes that the tale is set in what was then the present, adding to its immediacy. While effective tales of terror can still be set in the past – Susan Hill's *The Woman in Black*, for instance – modern work in the genre tends to use contemporary settings. Even if they've now been overtaken by nostalgia, writers such as M. R. James did at the time.

The narrator of 'The Rats in the Walls' is de la Poer, the surname of a branch of Poe's ancestry. He's 'a stolid Yankee' who has 'merged into the greyness of Massachusetts business life'. This justifies the sobriety of his narrative, but you may object that he hardly lives and breathes as a character; he isn't even allowed a first name. Even Lovecraft's most ardent admirers will admit that characterisation wasn't among his great strengths, but he developed a method that made this unnecessary, focusing on other aspects of the material. All the same, I'd argue that our narrator here is to some extent characterised by what he doesn't say. He expresses no grief over losing his injured son, and never even refers to the (deceased? estranged?) mother except to note her absence; we may conclude that he represses his emotions. Many manuals of composition recommend that writers should nurture every possible narrative skill; Stephen King's *On Writing* is a fine guide and more than that too – but you may also want to consider to what extent these skills enable you to convey and deal with your themes. Creative abilities aren't worth much if they're mechanically cultivated rather than growing organically out of the material.

The paragraphs that take us to Exham Priory maintain a light tone, the better to darken it later. The narrator's son is amused by the legends of the place, which is playfully portrayed as being 'perched perilously upon a precipice', the kind of alliteration Lovecraft's apprentice Robert Bloch (later to write *Psycho* along with much else) would make central to his witty style. The son's friend Edward Norrys, who will become crucial to the tale, is said to be 'a plump, amiable young man'. One word in that phrase will come back to haunt the narrative, and planting this kind of almost subliminal hint can be a powerful device. The apparently superstitious villagers – not a cliché in themselves when 'The Rats in the Walls' was written – regard the priory as 'a haunt of fiends and werewolves'. The hackneyed image both preserves the sense of rational disbelief that the accumulation of telling detail gradually undermines and prepares the way for darker revelations.

The mass of details in the next few paragraphs is artfully modulated; the subdued chronicle of the history of Exham is interspersed with hints about the family, which grow more evocative and sinister as they advance from indefinite 'fireside tales' to ballads that seem disturbingly specific, and then to tales that Lovecraft makes the narrator call 'hackneyed spectral lore'. In fact not all of them are hackneyed, so that the phrase serves to emphasise their vivid strangeness and, in retrospect, their accuracy. It's surely a measure of Lovecraft's restraint that we are almost a third of the way through the story before he introduces the first reference to the rats of the title. The sober chronicle of the ancestor who fled to America is just ominous enough to foreshadow later events.

Having established the background, the story starts to build up telling details in the present. Note how the pet cat's restlessness is described as trite – again, a way of delaying acceptance of its significance. Similarly, the cat's later behaviour and that of its companions is presented as 'picturesque' and accompanied by painterly images of architecture and lighting. By contrast, the narrator wakes into darkness from a nightmare rooted in the history of the place, and light shows him the first physical sign of the presence of the rats – or does it? Since nobody else has heard them, they could be a hallucination or proof that his senses are becoming bound up with his heritage.

As he and Norrys explore the sub-cellar they discover evidence of increasingly ancient practices; Lovecraft often uses such a progression to powerful effect. The two men keep a vigil in the cellar, and the narrator suffers a second nightmare whose climax and later significance is subtly hinted at: '… as I looked at these things they seemed nearer and more distinct—so distinct that I could almost observe their features. Then I did observe the flabby features of one of them—and awaked with such a scream that […] Capt. Norrys, who had not slept, laughed considerably. Norrys might have laughed more—or perhaps less—had he known what it was that made me scream…' (*Call*, pp100-101) The alert reader may also note that Norrys is also described as 'stouter' than his companion – another virtually subliminal detail that takes on a retrospective significance. During their vigil they learn that there is a vault below the sub-cellar. A progressive descent that reveals levels of new mystery is central to other Lovecraft tales – 'The Mound' and 'The Shadow out of Time', for instance.

Before the two men and a scientific party open the vault, the narrator has a third dream that sheds a sinister light on its predecessors without making the horror explicit. Lovecraft often allows the reader to anticipate on behalf of the protagonist, a method that can work just as well in horror as in tragedy, though it needs to be skilfully managed. Among the initial revelations is evidence that the passage to the vault was constructed from beneath the sub-cellar, a potently suggestive detail that's never explained. Does it imply that the de la Poer line was infiltrated by a subterranean race? In its inexplicability it helps the vault symbolise the narrator's subconscious – perhaps a hereditary one. At the sight of the contents of the vault Norrys appears to the narrator as 'plump […] utterly white and flabby' (Lovecraft 2002a: 104), while de la Poer himself utters inarticulate sounds, images that prefigure the climax. Even now, despite the occasional rhetorical outburst – 'Not Hoffmann or Huysmans could conceive a scene more wildly incredible, more frenetically repellent, or more Gothically grotesque than the twilit grotto through which we seven staggered' (Lovecraft 2002a: 105) – most of the prose keeps its composure; that is, the narrator apparently keeps his. It's only when he ventures into the unlit gulf beneath the vault that he and his language regress, reverting like the layers of history through which the exploration has led him and fulfilling his identification with his house.

The reversion is preceded by several lines of the kind of prose that is popularly identified as Lovecraftian. 'Then there came a sound from that inky, boundless, farther distance that I thought I knew; and I saw my old black cat dart past me like a winged Egyptian god, straight into the illimitable gulf of the unknown. But I was not far behind, for there was no doubt after another second. It was the eldritch scurrying of those fiend-born rats, always questing for new horrors, and determined to lead me on even unto those grinning caverns of Earth's centre where Nyarlathotep, the mad faceless god, howls blindly to the piping of two amorphous idiot flute-players.' I hope I've shown how carefully the culminating image here is prepared for, even within the paragraph; we may take the two Egyptian references as hinting at an occult correspondence between the horrors under Exham and ancient practices or legends elsewhere. In the dark he collides with 'something soft and plump', and the reader hardly needs the final paragraph to confirm what the narrator refuses to admit. The final line rises to a crescendo as lyrical as it is horrific, and preserves the ambiguity of the narrative without lessening its cumulative power. It's as though all the narrator's repressions burst forth in the last few paragraphs, overtaking even his language before he regains some imperfect control.

The entire tale was 'suggested by a very commonplace incident − the cracking of wallpaper late at night, and the chain of imaginings resulting from it.' Such are the ways of fiction writing, which can transform the initial idea out of all recognition. 'The Call of Cthulhu' (written in August or September 1926) was based on a dream, and Lovecraft recorded an element of the plot as early as 1919:

> Man visits museum of antiquities—asks that it accept a bas-relief *he has* just made—*old* and learned curator laughs & says he cannot accept anything so modern. Man says that
>
> 'dreams are older than brooding Egypt or the contemplative Sphinx or garden-girdled Babylonia'
>
> & that he had fashioned the sculpture in his dreams. Curator bids him shew his product, and when he does so curator shews horror. Asks who the man may be. He tells modern name. 'No—*before that*' says curator. Man does not remember except in dreams. Then curator offers high price, but man fears he means to destroy sculpture. Asks fabulous price—curator will consult directors. Add good development and describe nature of bas-relief. (Schultz, p.25)

Before considering the tale, let me note how important the opening lines are to the effect of many of his stories (while the final line of each is crucial, but to be appreciated in context rather than quoted here). Here are a few of the openings:

> Cautious investigators will hesitate to challenge the common belief that Robert Blake was killed by lightning, or by some profound nervous shock derived from an electrical discharge.
> − 'The Haunter of the Dark' (Lovecraft 2002a: 336)

You ask me to explain why I am afraid of a draught of cool air; why I shiver more than others upon entering a cold room, and seem nauseated and repelled when the chill of evening creeps through the heat of a mild autumn day.
– 'Cool Air' (130)

Bear in mind closely that I did not see any actual visual horror at the end.
– 'The Whisperer in Darkness' (200)

It is true that I have sent six bullets through the head of my best friend, and yet I hope to shew by this statement that I am not his murderer.
– 'The Thing on the Doorstep' (Lovecraft 2002c: 341)

I am forced into speech because men of science have refused to follow my advice without knowing why.
– 'At the Mountains of Madness' (Lovecraft 2002c: 246)

From a private hospital for the insane near Providence, Rhode Island, there recently disappeared an exceedingly singular person.
– 'The Case of Charles Dexter Ward' (Lovecraft 2002c: 90)

From even the greatest of horrors irony is seldom absent.
– 'The Shunned House' (Lovecraft 2002b: 90)

Other tales begin by setting the geographical scene; we'll see this in 'The Colour out of Space'. As for 'The Call of Cthulhu', it's one of those that begin with a statement of an aspect of Lovecraft's philosophy: 'The most merciful thing in the world, I think, is the inability of the human mind to correlate all its contents' (Lovecraft 2002a: 139). Mating science fiction and the occult, the tale is his first sustained essay in cosmic terror, founded in his sense of the indifference of the universe and of man's insignificance in space and time. Perhaps it's the scale of his theme that prompts him to make the narrative more persuasive by assembling documents that lead inexorably to the vast truth. The structure had already been used to lend conviction to fantastic and macabre tales; Wilkie Collins employed it in *The Moonstone*, and Stoker did in *Dracula*. While Lovecraft may have learned from at least the latter novel, the probable primary influence is Arthur Machen, who constructs 'The Great God Pan' along those lines (and who is referred to by name in the second chapter of Lovecraft's story). In 'The Call of Cthulhu' the method bears out the ominous vision of the opening paragraph.

Amid the sobriety of the first pages there are hints of menace, carefully restrained. The cause of Professor Angell's death is barely touched upon, but the reader is expected to pick it up. The nature of the bas-relief is lightly sketched to be developed later, though even so early there's a suggestion of wrongness. All the Providence and New Orleans locations are real, as is the earthquake, adding verisimilitude. The sculptor Wilcox's words to the professor are virtually identical to those Lovecraft told his correspondents that he spoke in his own original dream (one of the few details that figure unchanged in the tale). Given his wild dreams, the sculptor may seem to be a questionable witness of anything real, and the narrative withholds any endorsement of his account except by mentioning the professor's unusual interest in it. Lovecraft is reining his effects back, the better to release them where they'll be most telling, but he does include a hint of the size of the subject of Wilcox's dream. When the narrator begins to be swayed by the similarity of numerous other accounts, he's still inclined to blame some bias in the collection or interpretation of the data. By now, however, we're made to feel his skepticism may be unreasonable. It's an effective method of winning the reader over when used with skill, as here.

The second section of the narrative reveals the reasons for

Angell's obsession, all the more effectively for their having been delayed. It begins with a detailed description of the monster Wilcox sculpted. Even here, however, it's a sculpture that's described, which prefigures the eventual manifestation and allows Lovecraft not to go into such detail at the climax. I believe he may have learned this approach from M. R. James' ghost story 'Canon Alberic's Scrapbook', which Lovecraft had read in late 1925 and which uses the same technique; James also favoured complex structures, sometimes non-chronological, to achieve his effects. Early in this chapter Angell cites a further set of similarities, but these are more difficult to dismiss than the dreams, since they're authenticated by experts. Still, at this point they can be viewed merely as legends, the stuff of anthropology. Even the police inspector's account of the Louisiana ritual is challenged in a sense: the beliefs of the cultists are said to indicate 'an astonishing degree of cosmic imagination' although they 'might be least expected to possess it', a sentence in which skepticism is brought to bear and then subtly undermined.

It's worth examining the tone of Inspector Legrasse's account as given by the narrator. While the cult and its behaviour, together with the location, are described in evocative language, I don't think we're invited to assume that these are necessarily the policeman's words. (In 'The Space-Eaters', an early and intermittently very effective example of Lovecraft's influence, Lovecraft's friend Frank Belknap Long makes a policeman use this sort of language in direct speech, inadvertently undermining the credibility of the characterisation.) As a contrast, the paragraphs setting out the cult's beliefs are in plain prose – more accurately, a naïve voice, an effective method of conveying more than it openly states (a child's voice can be especially powerful). The quotation from the *Necronomicon* – the forbidden book that is one of Lovecraft's most famous inventions – recalls a verse from his minor 1920 tale 'Polaris', lines that refer to the Pole Star:

'Slumber, watcher, till the spheres
Six and twenty thousand years
Have revolv'd, and I return
To the spot where now I burn [...]
Only when my round is o'er
Shall the past disturb thy door.' (Lovecraft 2002b: 3-4)

'The Call of Cthulhu' develops this in terms of cosmic terror. I said earlier that his mythos was designed as an antidote to Victorian occultism, which he saw as excessively conventionalised and organised. Both the mythos and the *Necronomicon* were intended as partial glimpses of larger imaginative vistas, and it's regrettable that so many writers have sought to codify them.

The narrator's skeptical tone persists even in his visit to the sculptor Wilcox, but he can't entirely keep it up, given that he's aware of more than he has told us so far. As in 'The Rats in the Walls', the tone is invaded by expressions of repressed material. The final chapter starts by introducing the first document to be quoted in full, the newspaper clipping. While the report exemplifies reticence, a couple of suggestive phrases lie low amid the sober journalism. The last and most damning item, the Norwegian sailor's reminiscence, is paraphrased, which allows Lovecraft to modulate the language, so that the circumstantial detail of the opening sentences soon gives way to lyrical evocations of terror. Some of the descriptions of the island strongly recall 'Dagon', but in terms of the vision Lovecraft has now developed and expanded.

There's also a recurrence of one of his most potent effects – the vista or object that despite its ability to disturb only hints at greater and more terrible secrets hidden beyond or beneath. I'd suggest that part of the power of this image derives, as in 'The Rats in the Walls', from symbolising the unconscious; in 'The Call of Cthulhu', of course, it's actually the source of dreams. I should add that there's no need for Lovecraft to have intended the symbolism; sometimes in fiction the most eloquent material is partly unconscious, an unintended effect of telling the tale. The mythic echoes in the revelation of the monster are more conscious – certainly the references to the Cyclops, and the lethal effect of looking back is an equally resonant image from myth. The reference to an occurrence 'that the chronicler would not put on paper' may seem typically Lovecraftian, but it has its origins in Kipling, who uses the technique twice in his horror story 'The Mark of the Beast'. Like 'The Rats in the Walls', the present tale eventually but briefly bursts into delirious prose – 'There is a sense of spectral whirling through liquid gulfs of infinity, of dizzying rides through reeling universes on a comet's tail, and of hysterical plunges from the pit to the moon and from the moon back again to the pit, all livened by a cachinnating chorus of the distorted, hilarious elder gods and the green, bat-winged mocking imps of Tartarus' – which is indeed a dream or a delirium. The last paragraphs do their best to recapture control, first in Johansen's coda and then the narrator's, but this can't overcome the cumulative effect of the tale, which may be said to employ conspiracy paranoia before the tendency became fashionable.

'The Colour Out of Space' (written in March 1927) continues the evolution of Lovecraft's tales of terror towards science fiction. Later stories – 'At the Mountains of Madness', 'The Whisperer in Darkness', 'The Shadow out of Time' – take this further, but in 'Colour' he finds his single purest symbol of the otherness of the universe.

Hints of strangeness are woven into even the topographical realism of the opening paragraphs. The reference to 'the hidden lore of old ocean, and all the mystery of primal earth' (Lovecraft 2002a: 170) may resonate with readers of Lovecraft's earlier tales, but the images are delicate enough not to breach the understatement of the prose at this stage of the narrative. One way in which the scene-setting delays the full effect of the location is by holding it at a kind of aesthetic distance, with a theatrical reference ('the blasted heath') and a painterly one to Salvator Rosa. Just the same, there's a pronounced impression of wrongness, and the repetition of 'the blasted heath' is followed by a description that reinvents the image. (As S. T. Joshi has pointed out, the phrase is both theatrical and poetic, having been used by Milton as well as Shakespeare.) The paragraph includes two images that will gather significance later: the 'yawning black maw of an abandoned well whose stagnant vapours played strange tricks with the hues of the sunlight' and, more subtly, the 'odd timidity about the deep skyey voids above' with which the place infects the unnamed narrator.

Like 'The Call of Cthulhu' and other Lovecraft tales, the main text of 'The Colour out of Space' is a story paraphrased by the narrator, which helps Lovecraft to control the tone and gives the reader the option of suspecting, at least to begin with, that the narrator's reconstruction of events may be unreliable. The meteorite and its effects are initially described in simple but evocative language (indeed, evocative because simple), which is followed by several paragraphs of scientific analysis that don't dissipate the sense of strangeness. A crucial event – the releasing of part of the contents of the meteorite – is shown with such reticence it's almost comical: 'it burst with a nervous little pop.' Again, the unnatural destruction of the meteorite is presented in purely scientific and meteorological terms, but all these details are being amassed towards conveying unease without acknowledging any reason for it. It's a case of letting the reader suspect worse than has been put into the words.

The first stages of the influence of the alien presence are very lightly conveyed. Nahum Gardner finds his work more tiring than formerly and blames his age. Lovecraft constructs many of his paragraphs towards a climactic sentence – in this case muted in its effect, but elsewhere (as in the lyrical passages I've quoted earlier) closer to classical musical structure. The new crop of fruit shows an 'unwonted gloss', recalling the appearance of the meteorite. The alien taint begins to transform the wildlife, and despite the scientific reasons, the effects and the descriptions of them are oddly reminiscent of passages in George Macdonald's *The Princess and the Goblin*, a Victorian fairy tale in which animals have been mutated by magical influences; Lovecraft's increasing use of science in his fiction doesn't expunge the occult and fantastic but often embraces them, drawing on the imaginative strengths of both. The scientists who conducted the initial investigations of the meteorite now rationalise the effects around the Gardner farm, but the reader may well know better, although when the tale was written this dichotomy (between rationalists and some macabre truth) was less familiar in the genre. Employed skilfully, it can still work, and decades later Nigel Kneale made witty use of it in *Quatermass and the Pit*, a highly Lovecraftian piece.

The next few paragraphs grow oppressive with ominous details, psychological as well as physical. The first overt hints of something supernatural – the trees that move in no wind – are buried in the midst of paragraphs rather than dramatically placed at the end. Lovecraft may have learned this technique of unobtrusiveness in the layout of the material from M. R. James, who often uses this to startling effect (beware *Curious Warnings*, a recently edited edition of James that breaks down the paragraphs into shorter sections). Even when madness overtakes the Gardner family the language stays resolutely sober, except in the fragments of the mother's ravings. The hideous death of a family member is described by analogy with an earlier event, a reticent approach that I think adds to the horror.

The central section of the tale gives up detachment at last, with the informant Ammi Pierce's visit to the Gardner farm. The language only very gradually mounts to a pitch of physical horror, meanwhile subtly consolidating the hints of conscious alien activity around the farm (though even this is deftly qualified by the line 'a buggy-wheel must have brushed the coping and knocked in a stone', which we're free to take at face value if we like, but not for long). The language reaches a crescendo with the scene of Nahum's death, particularly his monologue. In *On Writing* Stephen King describes Lovecraft as 'a genius when it came to tales of the macabre, but a terrible dialogue writer,' and cites this monologue as proof. Is it, though, when taken in context? After all, it's a report by the narrator of what Ammi Pierce (described at the outset as 'rambling' with a mind that has 'snapped a trifle') recalled nearly 50 years later. I think Lovecraft uses it as a way of modulating the tone of the narrative rather than as literal dialogue. King objects that it consists of 'carefully constructed elliptical bursts of information', but it reminds me oddly of the gasping voices we find in Samuel Beckett's later plays and prose. I can also report that I've read the whole story aloud to an audience and made Nahum's monologue work perfectly well.

As soon as Pierce flees the Gardner farm the prose reverts to sobriety, preparing for the final climax. Having progressed through understatement to gruesomeness, the story will reach for awe ('wonder and terror', as Fritz Leiber puts it). Unadorned prose and a scrap of rustic dialogue – more properly, another monologue – give way to ornate evocative language as the manifestations become unambiguous. Even so, just as in the previous two stories I've looked at here, delirious images are kept to a single sentence: 'It was a monstrous constellation of unnatural light, like a glutted swarm of corpse-fed fireflies dancing hellish sarabands over an accursed marsh' (pp.193-194). The later passage that describes the 'riot of luminous amorphousness' performed by the colour recalls Mrs Gardner's ravings, since the language consists very largely of verbs – a way of preserving suggestiveness while offering vividness.

To what extent may Lovecraft have been aware how Freudian some of the images of the well are? In 1921 he commented 'We may not like to accept Freud, but I fear we shall have to do so.' I suspect he would have repudiated any sexual reading of the investigation of the well, simply because it detracts from the sense of awe and terror he wants to convey. Such readings can be useful if they enrich a text, and for some readers they may do here. The disturbance of the well begins the upsurge of language and imagery that is rounded off by an ominous diminuendo, Pierce's glimpse of a trace of the colour that returns to the well. Form and content are one throughout the whole climactic scene. The extended coda sinks into language that is mostly plain, but of course this has gained resonance from the entire narrative – even such an unemphatic phrase as 'the splotch of grey dust'. However, Lovecraft uses one extraordinary verbal trick, repeating word for word the narrator's sentence about his own timidity from the opening scene. Some of the final lines might almost be trying to reduce the significance of the alien visitation, but the tale is surely proof against that. 'It was just a colour out of space', but it epitomises Lovecraft's vision at least as powerfully as his mythos.

Since his death in 1937 Lovecraft has emerged as one of the most important writers in the field, and a pervasive influence. He both drew on the strengths of the authors he most admired – Poe, Algernon Blackwood (whose tale 'The Willows', with its evocation of absolute alienness, Lovecraft regarded as the greatest in the field), Arthur Machen, with his melding of Victorian science and the occult, and his sense of fairy tales and legends as metaphors for darker truths – and sought to improve on their limitations, as Lovecraft saw them. His ability in his best work to suggest terrors larger than he shows is as important as his attention to the power of language. While he wasn't averse to conveying 'loathsome fright', his most lasting legacy is the sense of mingled wonder and dread. His influence has been celebrated by a remarkable variety of writers; besides those I named at the outset, consider Alan Moore, Jorge Luis Borges, Stephen King, Thomas Pynchon, Mark Samuels, Caitlín Kiernan, China Miéville, Laird Barron... Artists as different as H. R. Giger and John Coulthart have drawn inspiration from him, and directors such as Roger Corman, Sean Branney and Stuart

Gordon have filmed his tales. His importance as a writer has been recognised by both the Library of America and Penguin Modern Classics, and the Penguin editions offer definitive restored texts. May his positive qualities continue to enrich literature! Horror fiction is much the better for them.

Ten Essential Stories

'Dagon' (July 1917)★
'The Rats in the Walls' (August–September 1923)★
'The Call of Cthulhu' (1926)★
'The Colour Out of Space' (March 1927)★
'The Outsider' (1921)
'The Music of Erich Zann' (1921)
'The Festival' (1923)
'Pickman's Model' (1926)
'The Thing on the Doorstep' (21-24 August 1933)
'The Haunter of the Dark' (November 1935)

Simon Van Booy

on

F. Scott Fitzgerald

I HAVE ACCIDENTALLY been haunting the life of F. Scott Fitzgerald for years. I live in the city where Fitzgerald set many of his important works, and am writing this in a century old New York City brick building, several stories above streets that still vibrate with the same nervous energy of traffic, food carts, and people shouting. I drive my daughter to school along the same notorious stretch of road, Northern Boulevard – where Fitzgerald's most famous character Jay Gatsby rattled into Manhattan from his mansion on the north shore of Long Island – and where his femme fatale struck and killed the poor mechanic's wife. Northern Boulevard is now just an endless patchwork of convenience stores, fast-food restaurants, and petrol stations, but somehow desolate in its frenzy, and equally as bleak as Fitzgerald's 'valley of ashes' that it replaced. At least once a week, I hurry past the cathedral on Fifth Avenue, where in 1920, a young F. Scott Fitzgerald married a southern socialist, Zelda Sayre, following the sale of *This Side of Paradise*.

Like many of the plots in his short stories, Zelda wouldn't marry Fitzgerald at first. Not only did her parents disapprove of the young Yankee, who was about to be shipped over to France to fight in World War I – but he was penniless. However, it's probably a myth that Zelda wanted to wait until

175

Fitzgerald was rich and famous before saying yes, because when they tied the knot, it was only a week after the publication of his first novel. And she was almost certainly defying her parents' wishes in becoming his wife.

If you come to New York in search of the ghosts from Fitzgerald's stories, you won't be disappointed. A writer once wrote that while Paris is the most modern of ancient cities, New York is the most ancient of modern cities. This is quite true. It doesn't take much exploring to find buildings crumbling from the inside. Original wall mouldings, antique door handles, and turn-of-the-century radiators have been painted over so many times – their age, swollen beneath white semi-gloss, is glaringly obvious. Many operating lifts still have wooden panelling and mechanical levers. In a city where landmark buildings have been famously torn down overnight, by some miracle, you can still catch glimpses of the roaring twenties through architectural remnants such as a corridor of tiles, once a covered walkway to The Biltmore Hotel (now the ceiling of an underground car park). There's even a chemist's shop in Brooklyn, housed in a former Vaudeville/silent film theatre, where it seems only the seats were ripped out to make room for toilet paper, cough syrup, and stationary. Certain bars near the East River claim to have discovered old tunnels leading to the water that were used during prohibition to smuggle in liquor.

One reason why the stories of F. Scott Fitzgerald are still very much alive today however, is the fact that modern Americans still wrestle with ideas of class and status – themes that Fitzgerald addressed in most of his short stories.

I came to Fitzgerald's work in my early thirties. Americans reel at my late appreciation of their national treasure – and it's true, here, Fitzgerald is a literary institution. His books are spread across American school and university curricula nationwide. When I first dipped into his work, it only took a few paragraphs before I was utterly hypnotized with his prose style.

Fitzgerald begins most of his short stories with an impressive show of force. By the time we meet the characters, we are already invested in what's going to happen to them. In 'May Day', the rich lyricism and sincerity (brilliantly shadowed by irony) of Fitzgerald's opening paragraph is immediately engaging:

> There had been a war fought and won and the great city of the conquering people was crossed with triumphal arches and vivid with thrown flowers of white, red, and rose. All through the long spring days the returning soldiers marched up the chief highway behind the strump of drums and the joyous, resonant wind of the brasses, while merchants and clerks left their bickerings and figurings and, crowding to the windows, turned their white-bunched faces gravely upon the passing battalions.
> – 'May Day' (Fitzgerald 2005: 122)

In some of his early works, the language that Fitzgerald uses to set up a story can even feel slightly overwritten:

> Trees filtering light onto dappled grass. Trees like tall, languid ladies with feather fans coquetting airily with the ugly roof of the monastery. Trees like butlers, bending courteously over placid walks and paths. Trees, trees over the hills on either side and scattering out in clumps and lines and woods all through eastern Maryland, delicate lace on the hems of many yellow fields, dark opaque backgrounds for flowered bushes or wild climbing gardens.
> – 'Benediction' (4)

Later on however, the prose settles into classic, pure, electrifying Fitzgerald:

She felt her soul recede suddenly from Kieth's. This was her brother – this, this unnatural person. She caught herself in the act of a little laugh.
– 'Benediction' (14)

Jim was born in a white house on a green corner.
– 'The Jelly-Bean' (173)

It's worth noting that the Fitzgeralds were quite famous in their own lifetimes, as appointed voices of the 1920s 'flapper' generation. He and his wife were celebrities, and although he takes credit for being the artist, time may eventually reveal the brilliant work of Zelda. Together they captured the changing attitudes of a generation, views that would eventually pervade the national consciousness and become mainstream. Fitzgerald also exposed the darker adjuncts of meritocracy through his descriptions of rampant industrialism, overnight wealth, glamour, and social pressure to maintain the appearance of decency – even if it meant corruption. One should also note that Fitzgerald's work would probably have been perceived as shocking by many of his readers, in the way his characters cast aside conventional views of relationships and openly relished casual, sexual encounters.

They stared at each other across the breakfast-table for a moment. Misty waves were passing before Bernice's eyes, while Marjorie's face wore that rather hard expression that she used when slightly intoxicated undergraduates were making love to her.
– 'Bernice Bobs Her Hair' (75)

Fitzgerald published widely in magazines such as *The Saturday Evening Post, Metropolitan,* and *The Smart Set.* Although his first novel in 1920 was a huge hit, Fitzgerald didn't earn much money from it. Its success however, helped drive up the price for his short stories.

'Bernice Bobs Her Hair' appeared in *The Saturday Evening Post* in 1920 about a month after his wedding in New York to Zelda. In this story, Fitzgerald unfolds the lives of two fifteen-year-old cousins. Bernice is visiting her cousin Marjorie, who is one of the most popular girls in town. Bernice is considered 'boring' by Marjorie's modern standards, and one morning the truth comes out; Marjorie explains to Bernice how dull everyone thinks she is and that she should go home if she's not prepared to have a good time. After a brief show of pride, Bernice asks Marjorie's advice about how to increase her popularity, and later on announces to a group of teenagers over dinner that she intends to 'bob' her hair. In the 1920s, bobbed hair was a glaring symbol of rebellion for women.

If the independent and willful female characters of Louisa May Alcott's *Little Women* left Victorian patriarchs aghast and set the standard of behavior for women in the nineteenth century – Fitzgerald's female characters, often rich, boozy, beautiful, and lost, gave women of the 1920s a chance to cross yet another boundary imposed upon them by society. In many of Fitzgerald's short stories – women openly fail, and admit their failure to themselves and to society.

'Do you want me to go home?'

'Well,' said Marjorie, considering, 'I suppose if you're not having a good time you'd better go. No use being miserable.'

'Don't you think common kindness–'

'Oh, please don't quote 'Little Women'!' cried Marjorie impatiently. 'That's out of style.'

'You think so?'

'Heavens, yes! What modern girl could live like those inane females?'

'They were models for our mothers.'

Marjorie laughed.

– 'Bernice Bobs Her Hair' (76)

Most of Fitzgerald's heroines are young, physically attractive southern belles, whose impulsiveness and material ambition, through marriage, are at odds with their fierce intelligence and longing for the sort of independence women enjoy today.

> Vaguely she wondered why she did not cry out that it was all a mistake. It was all she could do to keep from clutching her hair with both hands to protect it from the suddenly hostile world. Yet she did neither. Even the thought of her mother was no deterrent now. This was the test supreme of her sportsmanship; her right to walk unchallenged in the starry heaven of popular girls.
> – 'Bernice Bobs Her Hair' (86)

Often, characters yearn to escape the intellectually *less inclined* south, but cannot detach themselves from the loving, close-knit communities where they cherished long, slow childhoods. In 'The Ice Palace', Sally Carrol travels to a northern state to visit the family of a man she intends to marry:

> At first the Bellamy family puzzled her. The men were reliable and she liked them; to Mr. Bellamy especially, with his iron-gray hair and energetic dignity, she took an immediate fancy, once she found out that he was born in Kentucky; this made of him a link between the old life and the new. But toward the women she felt a definite hostility. Myra, her future sister-in-law, seemed the essence of spiritless conventionality. Her conversation was so utterly devoid of personality that Sally Carrol, who came from a country where a certain amount of charm and assurance could be taken for granted in the women, was inclined to despise her.
> – 'The Ice Palace' (57)

Sally Carrol eventually flees back home to Tarleton, Georgia, where she resumes her slow, southern lifestyle. Characters like Sally Carrol are drawn by Fitzgerald with such effortless charm, that even when they behave badly, or disappoint us, it is still difficult not to like them:

> …Sally Carrol smiled and blinked.
>
> 'Good mawnin'.'
>
> A head appeared torturously from under the car-top below.
>
> ''Tain't mawnin', Sally Carrol.'
>
> 'Sure enough!' she said in affected surprise. 'I guess maybe not.'
>
> 'What you doin'?'
>
> 'Eatin' green peach. 'Spect to die any minute.'
>
> – 'The Ice Palace' (66)

At the heart of Fitzgerald's short stories, one hears the thumping of real hearts. Whether he based most of his characters on people he knew, or created them from his imagination (likely a mix), Fitzgerald has an almost supernatural ability to bring characters to life on the page. This occurs in part by the way he shares so much of who his characters are through subtle, physical details:

> She was about nineteen, slender and supple, with a spoiled alluring mouth and quick gray eyes full of a radiant curiosity. Her feet, stockingless, and adorned rather than clad in blue-stain slippers which swung nonchalantly from her toes, were perched on the arm of a settee, adjoining the one she occupied. And as she read she intermittently regaled herself by a faint application to her tongue of a half-lemon that she held in her hand. The other half, sucked dry, lay on the deck at her feet and rocked very gently to and fro at the almost imperceptible motion of the tide.
>
> – 'The Offshore Pirate' (92)

And Fitzgerald's characters, both male and female, are almost always caught up in the tragic dichotomy between wealth and love. In this next passage from 'Winter Dreams', he explores the theme that made him famous:

> And so while he waited for her to appear he peopled the soft deep summer room and the sun porch that opened from it with the men who had already loved Judy Jones. He knew the sort of men they were – the men who when he first went to college had entered from the great prep-schools with graceful clothes and the deep tan of healthy summer, who did nothing or anything with the same debonair ease.
>
> Dexter had seen that, in one sense, he was better than these men. He was newer and stronger. Yet in acknowledging to himself that he wished his children to be like them he was admitting that he was but the rough, strong stuff from which this graceful aristocracy eternally sprang.
> – 'Winter Dreams' (239)

Americans today base class solely on wealth, and widely believe that anybody can be upper class if they earn enough money. The idea of the American Dream is a fantasy that has pulled immigrants from all parts of the world, and continues to today. For those who wish to dismiss the romantic idea of 'rags to riches', first consider people like Charlie Chaplin, who spent most of his childhood in desperate poverty (often homeless) in the slums of East London. Consider also, the current president, Barack Obama, raised in a single-parent household of modest means. Fitzgerald's male characters often achieve great success on their own merit, but then fail to appreciate it – preoccupied somehow with some earlier Romantic vision, impossibly out of their reach. Consider Dexter in the story 'Winter Dreams', who may have been an early version of Jay Gatsby:

Suddenly she turned her dark eyes directly upon him and the corners of her mouth drooped until her face seemed to open like a flower. He dared scarcely to breathe; he had the sense that she was exerting some force upon him, making him overwhelmingly conscious of the youth and mystery that wealth imprisons and preserves, the freshness of many clothes, of cool rooms and gleaming things, safe and proud above the hot struggles of the poor.
– 'Winter Dreams' (241)

Even after achieving great wealth and status, many of Fitzgerald's male and female characters (including Dexter), remain in despair, unable to connect emotionally or to settle down in the cool domestic life that is expected of them:

She took him in her roadster to a picnic supper and after supper she disappeared, likewise in her roadster, with another man. Dexter became enormously upset and was scarcely able to be decently civil to the other people present. When she assured him that she had not kissed the other man he knew she was lying – yet he was glad that she had taken the trouble to lie to him.
– 'Winter Dreams' (242)

The behavior of characters such as Judy Jones from 'Winter Dreams', and Nancy Lamar from 'The Jelly-Bean' bears a resemblance to the lives of certain young, modern, female celebrities.

For an instant her arms were around his neck – her lips were pressed to his.

'I'm a wild part of the world, Jelly-bean, but you did me a good turn.'

Then she was gone, down the porch, over the cricket-loud lawn.
– 'The Jelly Bean' (186)

And the main character in 'The Jelly-Bean' feels the stir of ambition through an unobtainable romance, common to Fitzgerald's male protagonists:

> So Nancy Lamar was going to marry. This toast of a town was to become the private property of an individual in white trousers – and all because white trousers' father made a better razor than his neighbor. As they descended the stairs Jim found the idea inexplicably depressing. For the first time in his life he felt a vague and romantic yearning.
> – 'The Jelly Bean' (179)

Characters like Jim from 'The Jelly Bean', Dexter from 'Winter Dreams', and Jay Gatsby are similar to characters in British Romantic literature, such as Pip from *Great Expectations* and Heathcliff from *Wuthering Heights.*

Heathcliff is rejected by Cathy because he is poor, uneducated, and working class. Although it's clear she loves him deeply, and is only amused by Edgar Linton, Linton is the wealthiest bachelor in the area, and Cathy marries him. Heathcliff disappears for a number of years and returns educated, finely dressed, and wealthier than anyone else in the vicinity. In a futile effort to win Cathy back, he makes everyone's life miserable (including in his own).

> He loved her and he would love her until the day he was too old for loving – but he could not have her. So he tasted the deep pain that is reserved only for the strong, just as he had tasted for a little while the deep happiness.
> – 'Winter Dreams' (249)

In his own life, Fitzgerald married the woman he fell in love with, and despite fame, creative genius, and their international recognition as symbols of the Jazz Age, their lives were not happy ones – often fraught with the sorts of issues his characters faced: infidelity, debt, and alcoholism.

Life did not end well. Fitzgerald died of a heart attack in his forties, and Zelda was killed a few years later when the mental hospital she was living in caught fire.

There are very few happy endings in Fitzgerald's short stories. His characters often depart the page through suicide, murder, or with terminal disappointment and resignation.

> 'Long ago,' he said, 'long ago, there was something in me, but now that thing is gone. Now that thing is gone, that thing is gone. I cannot cry. I cannot care. That thing will come back no more.'
> – 'Winter Dreams' (252)

The last few lines of 'Winter Dreams' remind me of the last paragraph of Joseph Conrad's novella, *Youth:*

> And we all nodded at him: the man of finance, the man of accounts, the man of law, we all nodded at him over the polished table that like a still sheet of brown water reflected our faces, lined, wrinkled; our faces marked by toil, by deceptions, by success, by love; our weary eyes looking still, looking always, looking anxiously for something out of life, that while it is expected is already gone – has passed unseen, in a sigh, in a flash – together with the youth, with the strength, with the romance of illusions. (Conrad, 63)

My favourite character from all of Fitzgerald's short stories is Bernice from 'Bernice Bobs Her Hair'.

> Softly she pushed open the door to Marjorie's room. She heard the quiet, even breathing of an untroubled conscience asleep.
> She was by the bedside now, very deliberate and calm. She acted swiftly. Bending over she found one of

the braids of Marjorie's hair, followed it up with her hand to the point nearest the head, and then holding it a little slack so that the sleeper would feel no pull, she reached down with the shears and severed it. With the pigtail in her hand she held her breath. Marjorie had muttered something in her sleep. Bernice deftly amputated the other braid, paused for an instant, and then flitted swiftly and silently back to her own room.

Down-stairs she opened the big front door, closed it carefully behind her, and feeling oddly happy and exuberant stepped off the porch into the moonlight, swinging her heavy grip like a shopping-bag. After a minute's brisk walk she discovered that her left hand still held the two blond braids. She laughed unexpectedly – had to shut her mouth hard to keep from emitting an absolute peal. She was passing Warren's house now, and on the impulse she set down her baggage, and swinging the braids like pieces of rope flung them at the wooden porch, where they landed with a slight thud. She laughed again, no longer restraining herself.

'Huh!' she giggled wildly. 'Scalp the selfish thing!'

Then picking up her suitcase she set off at a half-run down the moonlit street.

– 'Bernice Bobs Her Hair' (90-91)

In many ways, Bernice's cousin Marjorie is more typical of Fitzgerald's female characters. She is the wild girl, whom every boy wants to dance with, (like Judy Jones, Nancy Lamar, Sally Carrol, and Daisy Fay from *The Great Gatsby*). Bernice is somehow more self-realized, she bobs her hair, but then rebels against the set she has initiated herself into, perhaps not wishing to garner popularity through something so banal. In a few pages, Bernice goes from being a Victorian maid to a courageous, post-modern woman, and perhaps one of Fitzgerald's only characters who is not lost or disillusioned, bitter or indifferent.

While F. Scott Fitzgerald was famous for what his work stood for, and for bridging the Victorian and modern periods, I must admit that I truly admire his work as a reader, and adore his short stories as a writer. His short pieces are where he built strength as an author by experimenting with character, and gaining the courage to write simultaneously succinct and lyrical sentences. Reading his short stories is like listening to a musical genius rehearse and develop a piece of music that will later become an institution. F. Scott Fitzgerald's short stories are the training ground of genius.

Ten Essential Stories

'Bernice Bobs Her Hair' (1920)★
'The Ice Palace' (1920)★
'The Jelly-Bean' (1920)★
'Benediction' (1920)★
'The Off-Shore Pirate' (1920)
'Head And Shoulders' (1920)
'Winter Dreams' (1922)★
'May Day' (1922)★
'The Diamond As Big As The Ritz' (1922)
'Absolution' (1924)

Bibliography

INTRODUCTION

Anderson, Sherwood (1992) *Winesberg, Ohio*, London: Penguin.

Baldeshwiler, Eileen (1994) 'The Lyric Short Story: The Sketch of a History' in Charles E. May (ed.) *The New Short Story Theories*, Athens: Ohio.

Barthes, Roland (1980) *The Pleasure of the Text*, trans. Richard Miller, New York: Hill & Wang.

Doyle, Arthur Conan (1992) *The Adventures & Memoirs of Sherlock Holmes*, Ware: Wordsworth.

Levi, Mario (2011) *The Magic Paint*, London: Penguin.

Lovecraft, H.P. (2002) *The Call of Cthulhu and Other Weird Stories*, London: Penguin.

Marek, Adam (2008) *Instruction Manual for Swallowing*, Manchester: Comma.

Melville, Herman (2007) *Bartleby the Scrivener: A Tale of Wall Street*, London: Hesperus.

Nabokov, Vladimir (2001) *The Collected Stories*, London: Penguin.

Page, Ra (ed.) (2006) *Parenthesis*, Manchester: Comma

Poe, Edgar Allan (1993) *Tales of Mystery and Imagination*, Ware: Wordsworth.

Propp, Vladimir (1968) *Morphology of the Folktale*, trans Laurence Scott, intro Alan Dundes, Austen: University of Texas, 2nd Edition.

Stevick, Philip, ed. (1971) *The Anti-Story: an anthology of experimental fiction*, New York: Macmillan/Free Press.

BIBLIOGRAPHY

Nathaniel Hawthorne

Barthes, Roland (1980) *The Pleasure of the Text*, trans. Richard Miller, New York: Hill & Wang.

Hawthorne, Nathaniel (2008) *Young Goodman Brown and Other Tales*, Oxford: OUP.

Hawthorne, Nathaniel (1970) *The Scarlet Letter, and Selected Tales*, London: Penguin.

Carter, Angela (1982) *The Passion of New Eve*, London: Virago.

Marquez, Gabriel Garcia (2007) *One Hundred Years of Solitude*, London: Penguin.

Magrs, Paul (1997) *Does It Show?* , London: Vintage.

Magrs, Paul (1996) *Marked for Life*, London: Vintage.

Morrison, Ton (1997) *Beloved*, London: Vintage.

Rushdie, Salman (1998) *The Satanic Verses*, London: Vintage.

Edgar Allan Poe

Andersen, Hans Christian (1997) *The Red Shoes*, Watertown (MA): Charlesbridge.

Baudelaire, Charles (1995) *Selected Poems* from 'Flowers of Evil', trans by Wallace Fowlie, Mineola (NY): Dover.

Bowen, Elizabeth (1966) *The Demon Lover and Other Stories*, London: Penguin.

Browning, Robert (2000) *My Last Duchess and Other Poems*, Mineola (NY): Dover.

Coleridge, Samuel Taylor (2008) *The Major Works*, Oxford: OUP.

Dickens, Charles (2012) *The Cricket on the Hearth and Other Christmas Stories.* Mineola (NY): Dover.

Eliot, T.S. (1999) *Selected Essays,* London: Faber.

Fowles, John (2004) *The Collector*, London: Vintage.

Irving, Washington (2010) *Tales of a Traveler*, Whitefish (MO): Kessinger.

James, Henry (2000) *The Turn of the Screw.* Mineola (NY): Dover.

Poe, Edgar Allan (2009) *The Complete Egdar Allan Poe*, Ware: Wordsworth.

BIBLIOGRAPHY

Poe, Edgar Allan (2003) *The Fall of the House of Usher and Other Writings*, London: Penguin.

Poe, Edgar Allan (1993) *Tales of Mystery and Imagination*, Ware: Wordsworth.

Wilde, Oscar (1992) *The Picture of Dorian Gray*. Ware: Wordsworth.

Yeats, W.B. (1968) *Essays and Introductions*, London: Prentice Hall.

FYODOR DOSTOYEVSKY

Bakhtin, Mikhail (1984) *Problems of Dostoevsky's Poetics,* trans Caryl Emerson, Minneapolis: University of Minnesota Press.

Carver, Raymond (1993) *Where I'm Calling From: Selected Stories*, London: Harvill.

Dostoyevsky, Fyodor (2001) *The Best Short Stories of Fyodor Dostoevsky*, trans David Magarshack, New York: Modern Library.

Dostoyevsky, Fyodor (2003) *Crime and Punishment*, trans David McDuff, London: Penguin.

Dostoyevsky, Fyodor (2008) *The Eternal Husband and Other Stories,* trans. Pevear and Volokhonsky. New York: Bantam.

Dostoyevsky, Fyodor (1973) *Notes from the Underground, The Double*, trans Jessie Coulson, London: Penguin.

Dostoyevsky, Fyodor (1994) *A Writer's Diary,* Vol 1 1873-6, trans. Kenneth Lantz, London: Quartet.

Rogers, Jane (2000) *Island*, London: Abacus.

THOMAS HARDY

Brady, Kristin (1982) *The Short Stories of Thomas Hardy*, London: Palgrave MacMillan.

Hardy, Thomas (2009) *A Changed Man*, Fairfield (IO): Akaska Classics.

Hardy, Thomas (1993) *Far from the Madding Crowd*, Ware: Wordsworth.

Hardy, Thomas (2003) *The Fiddler of the Reels and Other Stories 1888-1900*, London: Penguin.

Hardy, Thomas (2009) *A Group of Noble Dames*, Fairfield (Iowa): Akaska Classics.

Hardy, Thomas (1996) *Life's Little Ironies,* Ware: Wordsworth.

Hardy, Thomas (1992) *Tess of the D'Urbervilles*, Ware: Wordsworth.

Hardy, Thomas (1999) *The Withered Arm and Other Short Stories*, London: Penguin.

Stewart, J.I.M (1971) *Thomas Hardy, A Critical Biography*, New York: Dodd, Mead & Co.

ARTHUR CONAN DOYLE

Doyle, Arthur Conan (1992) *The Adventures & Memoirs of Sherlock Holmes*, Ware: Wordsworth.

Collins, Wilkie (2003) *The Woman in White*, London: Penguin.

Doyle, Arthur Conan (2000) *The Supernatural Tales of Sir Arthur Conan Doyle*, ed. Peter Haining, London: Random (Gramercy).

Doyle, Arthur Conan (1985) *The Conan Doyle Stories*, New York: Hippocrene.

Doyle, Arthur Conan, (2003) *A Study in Scarlet,* Mineola (NY): Dover.

Doyle, Arthur Conan, (2001) *The Sign of Four*, London: Penguin.

Doyle, Arthur Conan, (2001) *The Valley of Fear* and Selected Srories, London: Penguin.

Doyle, Arthur Conan, (1994) *The Hound of the Baskervilles,* Mineola (NY): Dover.

Haddon, Mark (2004) *The Curious Incident of the Dog in the Night-Time*, London: Vintage.

Le Fanu, Sheridan (2009) *Uncle Silas*, Ware: Wordsworth.

Luckhurst, Roger, ed. (2009) *Late Victorian Gothic Tales*, Oxford: OUP.

Stevenson, Robert Louis (2013) *The Strange Case of Dr Jekyll and Mr Hyde and Other Tales of Terror*, London: Penguin.

BIBLIOGRAPHY

ANTON CHEKHOV

Chekhov, Anton (2008) *About Love and Other Stories*, trans. Rosamund Bartlett, Oxford: OUP.

Chekhov, Anton (1999) *The Essential Tales of Chekhov*, edited by Richard Ford, London: Granta.

Chekhov, Anton (2002) *The Lady with the Little Dog and Other Stories, 1896-1904*, London: Penguin.

Chekhov, Anton (2001) *The Steppe and Other Stories, 1887-91*, London: Penguin.

Chekhov, Anton (2002) *Ward No. 6 and Other Stories, 1892-1895,* London: Penguin.

De Maupassant, Guy (1997) *The Best Short Stories*, Ware: Wordsworth.

RUDYARD KIPLING

Karlin, Danny (1999) *Rudyard Kipling: the Oxford Authors*, Oxford: OUP.

Kipling, Rudyard (1994) *The Man Who Would Be King and Other Stories* (Wordsworth Classics) Ware: Wordsworth.

Kipling, Rudyard (2009) *Just So Stories* (Oxford World's Classics) Oxford: OUP.

Kipling, Rudyard (2001) *Selected Stories*, London: Penguin.

Kipling, Rudyard (1994) *Collected Stories*, London: Everymans.

H.G. WELLS

Alvarez, L. *et al* (1980) 'Extraterrestrial Cause for the Cretaceous-Tertiary Extinction' in *Science*, vol 208.

Aldiss, Brian and Wingrove, David (1986) *Trillion Year Spree*, London: Gollancz.

Baxter, Stephen (2008) *Flood,* London: Gollancz.

Clarke, Arthur C. (1973) *Rendezvous with Rama,* London: Gollancz.

Clarke, Arthur C. (1999) *Greetings, Carbon-Based Bipeds!,* London: HarperCollins.

Clute, John and Nicholls, Peter (1993) *The Encyclopaedia of Science Fiction*, London: Orbit.

BIBLIOGRAPHY

Flammarion, C. (1894) *Omega: The Last Days of the World,* Paris: Libraire-Editeur.

Foot, Michael (1995) *H.G.: The History of Mr Wells,* London: Doubleday.

Matthews, R.A.J. (1994) 'The Close Approach of Stars in the Stellar Neighbourhood' in *Quarterly Journal of the Royal Astronomical Society,* vol 35.

Pearson, Simon (2006) *A Brief History of the End of the World,* London: Robinson.

Smith, D. C. (1986) *H.G. Wells: Desperately Mortal,* New Haven: Yale.

Stapledon, Olaf (1931) *Last and First Men,* London: Methuen.

Verne, Jules (1877) *Hector Servadac* aka *Off on a Comet,* Paris: Hetzel.

Wells, H.G. (1897) 'The Star', *Graphic* Christmas number.

Wells, H.G. (2000) *The Complete Short Stories of H.G.Wells,* ed. John Hammond, London: Weidenfeld & Nicholson.

Wells, H.G. (2005) *The Time Machine,* introduction by Marina Warner, London: Penguin.

Wells, H.G. (2011) *HG Wells Classic Collection II: In the Days of the Comet, Men Like Gods, The Sleeper Awakes, The War in the Air,* London: Gollancz.

Wells, H.G. (2012) *The War of the Worlds,* London: Gollancz.

Wells, H.G. (2005) *The Island of Doctor Moreau,* introduction by Margaret Atwood, London: Penguin.

Wells, H.G. (2005) *The Invisible Man,* introduction by Margaret Atwood, London: Penguin.

Wylie, P. and Balmer, E. (1933) *When Worlds Collide,* New York: Stokes.

JAMES JOYCE

The Book of Acts, 8:9-24

Joyce, James. (2012) *Dubliners,* London: Penguin.

SHERWOOD ANDERSON

Anderson, Sherwood (1992) *Winesberg, Ohio,* London:

Penguin.

Anderson, Sherwood (2005) *The Triumph of the Egg*, Fairford (UK): Echo.

Anderson, S. (2006) *Death in the Woods and Other Stories,* London: W. W. Norton & Co.

FRANZ KAFKA

Auden, W.H. (1975) *The Dyer's Hand and Other Essays*, London: Faber.

Austen, Jane (1993) *Persuasion*, Ware: Wordsworth.

Benjamin, Walter (1968) *Illuminations,* London: Random.

Carroll, Lewis (1992) *Alice's Adventures in Wonderland & Through the Looking Glass*, Ware: Wordsworth.

Chekhov, Anton (2002) *The Lady with the Little Dog and Other Stories*, 1896-1904, London: Penguin.

Deleuze, Gilles and Guattari, Félix (1986) *Kafka: Toward a Minor Literature (Theory & History of Literature)*, Mineapolis: University of Minnesota Press.

James, Henry (2008) *The Ambassadors*, London: Penguin.

Kafka, Franz (2005) *The Complete Stories*, London: Vintage.

Kafka, Franz (2002) *The Great Wall of China and Other Short Works*, translated by Malcolm Pasley, London: Penguin.

Kafka, Franz (2000) *The Trial*, London: Penguin.

D.H. LAWRENCE

Lawrence, D.H. (2011) *Birds, Beasts and Flowers*, Bristol: Shearsman.

Lawrence, D.H. (1968) *The Complete Short Stories*. London: Heinemann, Phoenix Edition, vols I, II, III.

Lawrence, D.H. (1961) 'Morality and the Novel', in *Selected Literary Criticism*, edited by Anthony Beal, London: Heinemann.

Lawrence, D.H. (1962) *The Collected Letters of D. H. Lawrence*, edited by Harry T. Moore, London: Heinemann.

Lessing, Doris (1989) *The Golden Notebook,* London: Flamingo.

BIBLIOGRAPHY

Lowell, Robert (1988) *Interviews and Memoirs*, Ann Arbor: University of Michigan Press.

Worthen, John (1992) *D. H. Lawrence, The Early Years 1885-1912*, Cambridge: CUP.

KATHERINE MANSFIELD

Chekhov, Anton (2002) *The Lady with the Little Dog and Other Stories, 1896-1904*, London: Penguin.

Mansfield, Katherine (2007) *The Collected Stories*, London: Penguin.

Mansfield, Katherine (1930) *Novels and Novelists*, London: Constable and Constable.

Murry, John Middleton, ed. (1941) *The Letters of Katherine Mansfield*, New York: Knopf.

O'Sullivan, Vincent and Scott, Margaret, eds. (1984-1996) *The Collected Letters of Katherine Mansfield*. Four volumes. Oxford: OUP.

Scott, Margaret (2002) *Katherine Mansfield Notebooks: Complete Edition,* Minneapolis: University of Minnesota Press.

Tomalin, Claire (1987) *Katherine Mansfield: A Secret Life*, Penguin Books, London: Penguin.

Woolf, Leonard, ed. (1953) *A Writer's Diary: Being Extracts from the Diary of Virginia Woolf,* London: Hogarth.

H.P. LOVECRAFT

Blackwood, Algenon (1973) *Best Ghost Stories of Algernon Blackwood,* Mineola (NY): Dover.

Bloch, Robert (1978) *The Best of Robert Bloch*, New York: Ballantine.

Brite, Poppy Z (1996) *Wormwood*, London: Doubleday.

Campbell, Ramsey (2011) *The Inhabitant of the Lake and Other Unwelcome Tenants*, London: PS Publishing.

Collins, Wilkie (2002) *Moonstone*, Mineola (NY): Dover.

Hill, Susan (2012) *The Woman in Black: A Ghost Story.* London: Vintage.

James, M.R. (2005) *Count Magnus and Other Ghost Stories*

(*The Complete Ghost Stories of M. R. James, Vol. 1*) London: Penguin.

King, Stephen (2001) *On Writing*, London: Hodder.

Kipling, Rudyard (2005) 'The Mark of the Beast' in *Late Victorian Gothic Tales*, ed Roger Luckhurst, Oxford: OUP.

Klein, T.E.D. (1987) Dark Gods, London: Pan.

Kuttner, Henry (2009) Robots Have No Tails (Planet Stories Library) Redmond (WA): Paizo.

Leiber, Fritz (2011) *Selected Stories*, San Francisco: Night Shade.

Ligotti , Thomas (2008) Teatro Grottesco, London: Virgin.

Long, Frank Belknap (2000) 'The Space-Eaters', in *Tales of the Cthulhu Mythos* by H.P. Lovecraft and Others (intro James Turner). New York: Ballantine.

Lovecraft, H.P. (2002a) *The Call of Cthulhu and Other Weird Stories*, London: Penguin Modern Classics.

Lovecraft, H.P. (1986) *Dagon and Other Macabre Tales*, Saulk City (Winsconsin): Arkham House.

Lovecraft, H.P. (2002b) *The Dream in the Witch House and Other Weird Stories*, London: Penguin.

Lovecraft, H.P. (2004) 'Notes on Writing Weird Fiction' in *Collected Essays of H. P. Lovecraft: Vol 2: Literary Criticism*, ed. S. T. Joshi, New York: Hippocampus.

Lovecraft, H.P. (2004) 'Supernatural Horror in Literature' in *Collected Essays of H. P. Lovecraft: Vol 2: Literary Criticism*, ed. S. T. Joshi, New York: Hippocampus Press.

Lovecraft, H.P. (1995) *Miscellaneous Writings*, Saulk City (Winsconsin): Arkham House.

Lovecraft, H.P. (2002c) *The Thing on the Doorstep and Other Weird Stories*, London: Penguin.

MacDonald, George (2013) *The Princess and the Goblin, & The Princess and Curdie*. Ware: Wordsworth.

Machen, Arthur (2010) *The Great God Pan & The Hill of Dreams*, Seaside (OR): Watchmaker.

Schultz, David E. (ed) (1987) *H.P. Lovecraft: Commonplace Book*, West Warwick (RI): Necronomicon Press.

Stoker, Bram (2011) *Dracula*, Oxford: OUP.

Tem, Steve Rasnic, (1987) 'One View: Creating Character in Fantasy and Horror Fiction' in J. N. Williamson (ed.), *How to Write Tales of Horror, Fantasy & Science Fiction*, London: Robinson, pp35–41.

F. SCOTT FITZGERALD

Alcott, Louisa May (2008) *Little Women*, Oxford: Oxford World's Classics.

Bronte, Emily (1992) *Wuthering Heights*, Ware: Wordsworth.

Conrad, Joseph (2011) *Youth*, London: Penguin.

Dickens, Charles (1992) *Great Expectations*, Ware: Wordsworth.

Fitzgerald, F. Scott (2005) *The Best Early Stories of F. Scott Fitzgerald*, ed. Bryant Mangum, New York: The Modern Library.

Fitzgerald, F. Scott (1993) *The Crack-Up*, edited by Edmund Wilson, New York: New Directions.

Fitzgerald, F. Scott (1992) *The Great Gatsby,* Ware: Wordsworth.

Fitzgerald, F. Scott (2011) *This Side of Paradise,* Ware: Wordsworth.

Robuck, Erika (2013) *Call Me Zelda*, New York: Penguin.

Contributors

Brian Aldiss is one of the most important SF writers working in Britain today. He has published over 75 books, including the novels *Hothouse, The Interpreter, The Primal Urge, The Dark Light Years, The Billion Year Spree, The Helliconia Trilogy, Harm* and most recently *Walcot* (2009). His awards include the Hugo (twice), the Nebula, the Prix Jules Verne (Sweden), the Kurd Lasswitz Award (Germany), the John W. Campbell Memorial Award and three BSFA awards. Several of his books, including *Frankenstein Unbound*, have been adapted for the cinema, and his short story, 'Supertoys Last All Summer Long' was adapted by Stanley Kubrick and Steven Spielberg and released as the film *AI* in 2001. He is also a playwright, poet, editor and prolific short story writer.

Stephen Baxter's science fiction novels have won several awards including the John W Campbell Memorial Award, the British Science Fiction Association Award, the Kurd Lasswitz Award and the Seiun Award (all for *The Time Ships*), as well as the Philip K Dick Award (for *The Time Ships* and *Vacuum Diagrams*). He has published over 100 SF short stories, several of which have won prizes, including three Analog Awards, two BSFA awards and a Sidewise Award. His novel *Voyage* was dramatised by Audio Movies for BBC Radio and broadcast in 1999. His TV and movie work includes the BBC's *Invasion: Earth*, broadcast in April-May 1998, and Episode 3 of *Space Island One*, broadcast on Sky One in January 1998. His non-fiction includes the books *Deep Future* and *Omegatropic*. He is

President of the British Science Fiction Association, and a Vice-President of the H.G. Wells Society.

Simon Van Booy is the author of two collections of short stories, *The Secret Lives of People in Love* and *Love Begins in Winter*, which won the Frank O'Connor International Short Story Award. He has also written two novels, *Everything Beautiful Began After* and *The Illusion of Separateness,* and edited three philosophy books, *Why We Fight, Why We Need Love,* and *Why Our Decisions Don't Matter.* His essays have appeared in the *New York Times, The Times, The Guardian*, and *ELLE Men* (China). He has also written for the stage, National Public Radio, and the BBC. He teaches part-time at SVA in Manhattan, and is involved in the Rutgers Early College Humanities Program for young adults living in under-served communities. In 2013, he founded *Writers for Children,* an organization which helps young people build confidence in their talent, through annual writing awards. His work has been translated into more than sixteen languages.

Frank Cottrell Boyce is an award-winning screenwriter and children's novelist. His film credits include *Welcome to Sarajevo, Hilary and Jackie, Code 46, 24 Hour Party People, A Cock and Bull Story*, and most recently *The Railway Man*. In 2004, his debut novel, *Millions,* won the Carnegie Medal and was shortlisted for The Guardian Children's Fiction Award, and was followed by *Framed* (later adapted into a film by the BBC), *The Unforgotten Coat*, and three installments of the *Chitty Chitty Bang Bang* series. Frank also writes for the theatre and was the author of the highly acclaimed BBC film *God on Trial.* He has previously contributed stories to Comma's anthologies *Phobic, The Book of Liverpool, The New Uncanny, When It Changed,* and *Litmus* and is currently working on a full collection for Comma, *Triple Word Score*. He also wrote the script for the opening ceremony of the 2012 London Olympics.

Ramsey Campbell is described by the *Oxford Companion to English Literature* as 'Britain's most respected living horror writer', and in 1991 was voted the 'Horror Writer's Horror Writer' in *The Observer* Magazine. His many award-winning novels include *The Face That Must Die, Incarnate, The Overnight*, and *The Grin of the Dark*. He has also published sixteen collections of short stories to date, most recently *Told by the Dead* (2003), *Inconsequential Tales* (2008), *Just Behind You* (2009), and *Holes For Faces* (2013).

David Constantine has published several volumes of poetry, most recently, *Nine Fathom Deep* (2009). He is a translator of Hölderlin, Brecht, Goethe, Kleist, Michaux and Jaccottet. In 2003 his translation of Hans Magnus Enzensberger's *Lighter than Air* won the Corneliu M Popescu Prize for European Poetry Translation. His translation of Goethe's *Faust*, Part I was published by Penguin in 2005; Part II in April 2009. He is also author of one novel, *Davies*, and *Fields of Fire: A Life of Sir William Hamilton*. His three short story collections are *Back at the Spike*, the highly acclaimed *Under the Dam* (Comma, 2005), and *The Shieling* (Comma, 2009), which was shortlisted for the 2010 Frank O'Connor International Short Story Award. Constantine's story 'Tea at the Midland' won the BBC National Short Story Award 2010, and his fourth collection, by the same name, won the 2013 Frank O'Connor International Short Story Award.

Martin Edwards is an award-winning crime writer whose latest Lake District Mystery is *The Frozen Shroud*. The series includes *The Coffin Trail* (shortlisted for the Theakston's prize for best British crime novel), *The Arsenic Labyrinth* (shortlisted for the Lakeland Book of the Year award) and *The Serpent Pool*. He has written eight novels about Liverpool lawyer Harry Devlin, starting with *All the Lonely People*, and two stand-alone novels, including *Dancing for the Hangman*. He won the CWA Short Story Dagger in 2008, and has edited 21 anthologies of short stories, including *I.D. Crimes of Identity* and *M.O. Crimes of Practice* (both with Comma). He has also published eight non-fiction books. He is Archivist of the Detection Club and the Crime Writers' Association and is also a partner in a national law firm.

Stuart Evers was born in Macclesfield, Cheshire in 1976. His first book, *Ten Stories About Smoking* was published by Picador in 2011 and won The London Book Award. His short fiction has appeared in *Prospect, The Best British Short Stories 2012,* TheSundayTimes.co.uk, *The Reader* and *3:AM*, and he regularly writes about books for *The Guardian, The Independent, The Telegraph* and *The Observer. If This is Home* – his debut novel – was published by Picador in July 2012.

Toby Litt is the author of eight novels – *Beatniks: An English Road Movie, Corpsing, Deadkidsongs, Finding Myself, Ghost Story, Hospital, Journey into Space* and *King Death* – as well as three collections of short stories: *Adventures in Capitalism, Exhibitionism* and *I Play the Drums in a Band Called Okay.* In 2003 Toby Litt was nominated by Granta magazine as one of the 20 'Best of Young British Novelists'. His short story 'Call it "The Bug" Because I Have No Time to Think of a Better Title' was specially commissioned for Comma's *Bio-Punk* anthology and was shortlisted for the 2013 Sunday Times EFG Private Bank Short Story Prize.

Alison MacLeod's short fiction has been published in a wide range of magazines including *Prospect, London Magazine, The Sunday Times* online magazine, in anthologies such as *The New Uncanny, Litmus, The 2011 BBC National Short Story Award* (all Comma) and broadcast on the BBC. A story from her collection, *Fifteen Modern Tales of Attraction,* 'Dirty Weekend', was awarded the Society of Authors' Olive Cook Prize for Short Fiction. She is also the author of three novels,

The Changeling (1996), *The Wave Theory of Angels* (2005), and *Unexploded* (2013), which was longlisted for the Man-Booker Prize. She has won Writers' Awards from both Arts Council England and the Canada Council for the Arts. She is Professor of Contemporary Fiction at the University of Chichester and is currently completing her second short story collection.

Sara Maitland grew up in Galloway and studied at Oxford University. Her first novel, *Daughters of Jerusalem*, was published in 1978 and won the Somerset Maugham Award. Novels since have included *Three Times Table* (1990), *Home Truths* (1993) and *Brittle Joys* (1999), and one co-written with Michelene Wandor – *Arky Types* (1987). Her short story collections include *Telling Tales* (1983), *A Book of Spells* (1987) and most recently, *On Becoming a Fairy Godmother* (2003). Her non-fiction works include *The Book of Silence* and *Gossip from the Forest* (both Granta). Her latest collection is *Moss Witch* (Comma, 2013), a series of short stories inspired by conversations with leading scientists.

Sean O'Brien is Professor of Creative Writing at Newcastle University and has published seven poetry collections, including *The Drowned Book* which won both the Forward and TS Eliot prizes, and *November*. His *Collected Poems* was published in 2012. His translations include Dante's *Inferno*, Aristophanes' *Birds* and Zamyatin's *We*. He has also published a collection of essays, *The Deregulated Muse*, and a novel, *Afterlife*. He is a regular writer for the *TLS* and makes occasional contributions to the *Guardian* and *The Independent*. Sean's first full collection of short stories, *The Silence Room* was published by Comma in 2008. Short stories have since appeared in *Litmus*, *Lemistry*, and *Bio-Punk* (all Comma).

Adam Roberts was born in London two thirds of the way through the last century. He is a writer and academic, and lives a little way west of the city of his birth – fifteen miles or so. His latest books are *Jack Glass* (Gollancz 2012) and *Twenty Trillion Leagues Under the Sea* (Gollancz 2014). His short story collection *Adam Robots* was published in 2013.

Jane Rogers has written eight novels including *Mr Wroe's Virgins* (which she dramatised as an award-winning BBC drama serial), *Her Living Image* (Somerset Maugham Award), *Island,* and *Promised Lands* (Writers Guild Best Fiction Award). Her most recent novel *The Testament of Jessie Lamb* was longlisted for the 2011 Man-Booker prize, and won the Arthur C. Clarke Award 2012. Her short story collection, *Hitting Trees with Sticks* was shortlisted for the 2013 Edge Hill Award. She also writes radio drama and adaptations. She is Professor of Writing at Sheffield Hallam University and is a Fellow of the Royal Society of Literature.

Ali Smith was born in Inverness in 1962 and lives in Cambridge. Her first book, *Free Love*, won the Saltire First Book Award. She is also the author of *Like* (1997); *Other Stories and Other Stories* (1999); *Hotel World* (2001), which was shortlisted for both the Orange Prize and the Man Booker Prize in 2001 and won the Encore Award, the East England Arts Award of the Year, and the Scottish Arts Council Book of the Year Award in 2002; *The Whole Story and Other Stories* (2003); *The Accidental* (2005), which won the 2005 Whitbread Novel Award and was shortlisted for the Orange Prize and the Man Booker Prize; and *The First Person and Other Stories* (2008). She was also a recipient of the Arts Foundation Fellowship for the Short Story.